Essential
Canada
West

by Karen Pieringer and Fiona Malins

Above: *Snow-capped mountains, Yoho National Park*

AAA Publishing
1000 AAA Drive, Heathrow, Florida 32746

Detail of an Inuit carving at the Museum of Anthropology, Vancouver

Front Cover AA Travel Library/Pete Bennett: *Stanley Park's Brockton Point totem poles, Victoria* Back Cover AA Travel Library/Harold Harris: *Seaplane, Victoria harbour*

Written by Karen Pieringer and Fiona Malins

First published 2005.

Edited, designed and produced by AA Publishing
© Automobile Association Developments Limited 2005.

Automobile Association Developments Limited retains the copyright in the original edition © 2005 and in all subsequent editions, reprints and amendments.

The contents of this publication are believed correct at the time of printing. Nevertheless, the publishers cannot accept responsibility for errors or omissions or for changes in details given. We are always grateful to readers who let us know of any errors or omissions they come across, and future printings will be updated accordingly.

Library of Congress Catalog Card Number: on file

ISBN 1-59508-043-0

Published in the United States by AAA Publishing, 1000 AAA Drive, Heathrow, Florida 32746

Published in the United Kingdom by AA Publishing

A01997
Mapping produced from Canada data © Tele Atlas N.V. 2005.

Colour separation: Keenes, Andover
Printed and bound in Italy by Printers Trento S.r.l.

Find out more about AAA Publishing and the wide range of services that AAA provides by visiting our website at aaa.com

The weather chart on **page 118** of this book is calibrated in °C. For conversion to °F simply use the following formula:

$$°F = 1.8 \times °C + 32$$

Contents

About this Book

This book is divided into five sections to cover the most important aspects of your visit to the region.

Viewing Western Canada pages 5–14
An introduction to Western Canada by one of the authors.
Western Canada's Features
Essence of Western Canada
The Shaping of Western Canada
Peace and Quiet
Western Canada's Famous

Top Ten pages 15–26
The authors' choice of the Top Ten places to see in the region, listed in alphabetical order, each with practical information.

What to See pages 27–90
The four main areas of Western Canada, each with its own brief introduction and an alphabetical listing of the main attractions.
Practical information
Snippets of "Did you know…" information
5 suggested walks
4 suggested tours
3 features

Where To… pages 91–116
Detailed listings of the best places to eat, stay, shop, take the children and be entertained.

Practical Matters pages 117–24
A highly visual section containing essential travel information.

Maps
All map references are to the individual maps found in the What to See section of this guide.
For example, Victoria has the reference
✚ 50 B1 – indicating the page on which the map is located and the grid square in which the city is to be found. A list of the maps that have been used in this travel guide can be found in the index.

Prices
Where appropriate, an indication of the cost of an establishment is given by $ signs:

$$$ denotes higher prices
$$ denotes average prices
$ denotes lower charges.

Star Ratings
Most of the places described in this book have been given a separate rating:

✪✪✪ Do not miss
✪✪ Highly recommended
✪ Worth seeing

Viewing
Western
Canada

Above: *riding horseback is still one of the best ways of exploring Western Canada*

Fiona Mallins' Western Canada

Midnight Sun
It is not easy to get enough sleep when the sun never sets. Once, on Baffin Island, there was enough light to sit outside reading until 2am, even though the sun had dipped below the surrounding mountains. I finally slept, only to be awoken by the brilliant rays of the sun illuminating my bedroom – at 4.45am.

Below: *eagles are best seen during the fall salmon run*
Bottom: *Peyto Lake, one of the highlights of the Icefields Parkway*

Traveling in Western and Northern Canada is always a wonderful experience for me, and back in my big-city home in the East (Montréal), I often dream of those wide open spaces. Some people say the Prairies are monotonous, but to me they represent an exhilarating part of the journey westward, with their ever-changing rainbow of colors – fields of golden wheat, blue-flowered flax and yellow rape, dotted with tall brightly-painted grain elevators that are visible for miles around and sloughs (ponds) teeming with ducks and other birds.

Beyond Calgary the Rocky Mountains begin to loom large on the horizon, and anticipation increases with every view of their majestic peaks and the unbelievable colors of the lakes. Up here you cross into British Columbia – beautiful BC, as its residents modestly call it. Spectacular would not be overstating the case, with its wonderful coast and fabulous mountains. Vancouver has one of the most magnificent locations of any city on earth and Victoria's setting is only slightly less stunning. Both cities offer world-class museums and entertainments, but each has a distinct character: Vancouver blends a laid-back yet trendy atmosphere with superb shopping and a vibrant cultural scene; Victoria preserves a unique, cozy "Englishness" alongside the dignity of its provincial capital status.

Northern Canada is simply amazing, a vast wilderness with 24 hours of summer daylight, the grandiose Mackenzie River flowing into the Arctic Ocean, mountainous Baffin Island astride the Arctic Circle, and the wonders of the Yukon. To quote Robert Service, "I want to go back – and I will."

Western Canada's Features

Geography
- Population: 9 million.
- Greatest river: Mackenzie (1,800km/1,118 miles long).
- Biggest lakes: Great Bear (31,328sq km/12,100sq miles), Great Slave (28,568sq km/11,034sq miles), and Lake Winnipeg (24,387sq km/12,100sq miles). Great Slave is the deepest (614m/2,014ft).
- Highest peak: Mount Logan (5,950m/19,520ft).
- The Arctic archipelago is the largest group of islands in the world. The biggest is Baffin (▶ 85) at 507,451sq km (195,900sq miles).

Famous Products
- The West Coast First Nations are renowned for woodcarving and making jewelry and other items.
- Pacific salmon, caught offshore and in the rivers, are delicious, especially when smoked.
- The Okanagan Valley in BC is famous for fruit orchards and wineries (▶ 44).
- Alberta beef, grazed on prairie meadows, is supremely succulent.
- The Inuit produce evocative artworks, including carvings, lithographs and etchings (▶ 109).
- Yukon jewelers create beautiful pieces using local gold.

Animal Life
- The Western mountain ranges are the domain of moose, elk, deer, black and grizzly bears and a variety of sheep.
- Bison (North American buffalo) only roam freely within the Wood Buffalo National Park, but can also be viewed in paddocks at Elk Island, Prince Albert and Waterton Lakes (▶ 45).
- Off the West Coast, pods of migrating whales are often seen, along with the resident populations of orcas, seals, other sea mammals and a variety of birds.
- The bald eagle population of BC is set to overtake Alaska as the largest concentration in the world.
- Once nearly trapped out of existence, beavers have made a comeback and are now prolific in streams and lakes.

Sports and Activities
Opportunities for outdoor activities are limitless, with rivers and lakes for canoeing, rafting and fishing for trophy size northern pike, walleye, trout and grayling, plus sea kayaking and whale-watching on the coast. There are magnificent trails for hiking, mountain biking and horseback riding, and good golf courses. Winter sports are superlative in the mountains, and include snowmobiling, ice-fishing and sleigh rides, while armchair sports enthusiasts can thrill to the national obsession – hockey.

Above: *Canadians are passionate about hockey*
Below: *elk are prominent among western wildlife*

Essence of Western Canada

One of the first things to understand about this region is its enormous size. It is simply impossible to see it all. The choices it presents are equally immense – the grandeur of the Rocky Mountains and their iridescent lakes, the spectacular coastline of British Columbia, with its deep inlets and fjords battered by the ocean, the vast agricultural lands and cowboy culture of the Prairies, and the northern wilderness – land of midnight sun and northern lights – with wonderful wildlife and a small population who are determined to survive in the sometimes harsh environment.

Western Canada also has sophisticated urban centers such as cosmopolitan Vancouver, captivating Victoria, the vibrant cities of Edmonton and Calgary in Alberta and fascinating Winnipeg.

Below: *Vancouver's leafy Gastown area is full of restored 19th-century buildings*
Bottom: *the last rays of the setting sun glow through an Inuit sculpture on English Bay*

THE **10** ESSENTIALS

If you only have a short time to visit Western Canada, or would like to get a really complete picture of the region, here are the essentials:

• **Join in the excitement** of the chuckwagon races and the rodeo at the Calgary Stampede (► 72), or attend one of the many rodeo events in Prairies cowboy country.

• **Follow a trail** through Horseshoe Canyon near Drumheller (► 76), amid the stunning scenery of the Badlands of Alberta, world-famous as a dinosaur graveyard.

• **Travel west across Saskatchewan** from the Manitoba border for the full impact of the wide open spaces of the Prairies, with wheat fields stretching to the horizon beneath enormous skies that are full of stars at night.

• **Drive toward the Rockies** from Calgary, watching the wall of mountains get ever nearer as the plains dissolve beneath your wheels.

• **Walk to the base of Mount Edith Cavell** in Jasper National Park (► 20) and gaze up at the Angel Glacier, named for its two outstretched arms.

• **Wander along the shores** of any of the famous Rocky Mountain lakes and marvel at the remarkable color of the water (► 24).

• **Sit on the beach at sunset** in Pacific Rim National Park (► 56), watching the sun disappear beyond thousands of miles of ocean.

• **Stay up late** on the Arctic Circle at Pangnirtung on Baffin Island (► 85) in late June and enjoy the midnight sun, or time your visit to see the amazing displays of the aurora borealis, painting the sky with its dancing colored light.

• **Take a wildlife-spotting trip**, perhaps to view the polar bears at Churchill, Manitoba (► 74), on the shores of Hudson Bay, or to skim the waves amid pods of whales off the BC coast.

• **Walk the wooden boardwalks** of Dawson City (► 81), in the Yukon, and imagine the Gold-Rush fever that gripped the town a century ago.

Above: *whale-watching is a popular activity*

Below: *daredevil bronco buster in a Prairies rodeo*

9

The Shaping of Western Canada

13,000 years ago
Before the end of the last Ice Age, the first human beings arrive in Western Canada by land bridge from Siberia.

1576
In search of a northwest passage to the Orient, Englishman Martin Frobisher enters Baffin Island's Frobisher Bay.

1610–11
Entering the bay that now bears his name, Englishman Henry Hudson is abandoned by his crew.

1670
The Hudson's Bay Company is chartered by the English king to trade furs out of Hudson's Bay.

1770–72
While exploring the Northwest Territories, Hudson's Bay Company employee Samuel Hearne is the first European to reach the Arctic Ocean overland.

1778
James Cook explores the Pacific Coast for the British Navy, from Nootka Sound to the Bering Strait.

1792–94
George Vancouver, also with the British Navy, explores the coasts of mainland BC and Vancouver Island.

1789–93
Alexander Mackenzie, of the Northwest Company, descends the Mackenzie River to the Arctic Ocean. In 1793, he is the first European to cross the Rockies and reach the Pacific Coast (at Bella Coola) by land.

1808
Simon Fraser, also of the Northwest Company, descends the Fraser River to the Pacific (at what is now Vancouver).

1811
Financed by Lord Selkirk, Highland Scots establish the first European community in the Prairies (now Winnipeg).

This historic company is still trading, as "The Bay"

1843
James Douglas, of the Hudson's Bay Company, founds Victoria on Vancouver Island.

1858
Gold is discovered in the Fraser River, sparking the first Gold Rush. The colony of British Columbia is created.

July 1, 1867
In the East, Canada is officially created as a confederation of provinces.

1869–70
Under Louis Riel, the Métis revolt when the Hudson's Bay Company lands (now the Northwest Territories) are sold to the new Canada. They are crushed, but as a result the province of Manitoba is born in 1870.

1871
British Columbia joins Canada on the condition that a railroad be built to link it to the east.

1873
The Northwest Mounted Police force is created to keep order in Canada; in 1920 they become the Royal Canadian Mounted Police.

1880
The British Government transfers the Arctic to Canadian jurisdiction.

The railroad spanned the continent in the 1880s

1885
Again led by Louis Riel, the Métis revolt once more, this time in Saskatchewan, but are crushed by troops arriving on the new railroad.

November 7, 1885
The last spike of the Canadian Pacific Railway is driven at Craigellachie, British Columbia.

1886
Vancouver is founded as the western terminus of the railroad; the first Trans-Canada train arrives.

1896
Gold is discovered in the Yukon, sparking the Klondike Gold Rush and leading to the creation of Yukon Territory.

1905
The provinces of Alberta and Saskatchewan are carved out of the Northwest Territories.

1904
Roald Amundsen becomes the first person to successfully navigate the Northwest Passage.

1914–18
During World War I, 650,000 Canadians enlist and 60,000 are killed.

1939–45
In World War II, more than a million Canadians serve; 42,042 are killed and 54,414 wounded.

1965
Canada adopts the Maple Leaf flag.

Winnipeg in 1875

1967
The centenary of Canadian Confederation is celebrated right across the country.

1986
The Expo' 86 World's Fair is held in Vancouver.

1988
The Winter Olympic Games are held in Calgary.

1999
The Territory of Nunavut is carved out of the Northwest Territories for the Inuit, with a high degree of self-rule.

2004
Canada is rocked by the Sponsorship scandal. Millions of dollars put aside to promote the Federal government in Québec are misappropriated, forcing a federal election. The liberal party scrape back in, but with no seats held anywhere west of Manitoba.

Peace & Quiet

Canada is vast and yet the population is only about half that of the UK. Consequently, there are plenty of opportunities to get away from it all. Peace and quiet is as important to residents as it is to visitors, and most of the urban population own or frequently rent a weekend escape within comfortable driving distance of home. This means that the whole country is geared up to cater to this call of the wild, and it is relatively easy to find solitude.

National and Provincial Parks

The area covered by this book contains 21 national parks and countless provincial parks, reflecting the nation's concern for conservation and ecological awareness. The fame of Banff and Jasper national parks is widespread, which means they attract a great number of visitors in the summer months. It is, however, always possible to get away from the crowds by striking off the main roads and trails (details of all trails can be obtained from the national park offices), or by visiting other lesser known but still beautiful areas of the Rockies such as the Yoho valley in Yoho National Park, Mount Robson Provincial Park or Kootenay National Park in British Columbia.

The sun goes down behind dramatic sea stacks on the Pacific coast

In the Prairies, Manitoba's Riding Mountain National Park is a rolling plateau of wooded slopes and lakes above the surrounding plains. In Saskatchewan, the Prince Albert park lies at the point where the southern aspen forest turns to northern boreal, housing an incredible variety of wildlife. The Cypress Hills, spanning the Saskatchewan-Alberta border, offer a quiet retreat among tall lodgepole pines, wild flowers and bird song.

On Vancouver Island, the Pacific Rim National Park (► 56) includes rain forest, wild coastline and offshore islands, where you feel all alone with the ocean. In the center of the island, the Strathcona Provincial Park offers thousands of hectares of almost untouched wilderness.

Most parks have campgrounds and many have canoe and kayak rental and programs of ranger-led activities and hikes. For information visit www.pc.gc.ca or contact local tourist offices (► 120).

Peace in the Prairies

In addition to its parks, the Prairies have huge agricultural areas to explore on hiking, bicycling and horseback riding trails, and anglers can find remote rivers and lakes full of plump fish. Any study of

Manitoba quickly shows just how much of the province is made up of water. There are large bodies such as lakes Winnipeg and Manitoba and a wealth of smaller ones. Hecla Provincial Park in Lake Winnipeg has lush forests, rugged shores and lovely beaches, making it ideal for getting away from it all.

Top: *Emerald Lake, in Yoho National Park, is a perfect spot to unwind*
Above: *caribou, or North American reindeer, in the Yukon*

Inland British Columbia

If British Columbia means magnificent mountains and the wonderful Pacific coast to you, don't overlook the interior that lies between. This remarkable rolling plateau, covered with sagebrush and pierced by lakes, includes the lush Okanagan Valley (► 44), full of fruit orchards, vineyards and wineries, and the Cariboo – cattle-raising country where you can stay on a ranch and explore on horseback.

The North

The north – Yukon, Northwest Territories and Nunavut – offers a level of peace and quiet that is unequalled on earth. Advanced survival skills are needed to explore the difficult terrain of this wild country, but it is possible to join excursions organized by experienced outfitters to explore such areas as the glorious wilderness of Nahanni National Park (► 88) or the glacier-scarred landscape of Auyuittuq on Baffin Island (► 85).

Western Canada's Famous

Western Canadian musicians who have enthralled an international audience include Bryan Adams (top) and Diana Krall (above)

Music and Dance

Western Canada has contributed a number of pop stars to the world. Vancouver's Bryan Adams still holds the record for the longest running number-one single in pop history, "Everything I Do, I Do It For You" (1991), and GRAMMY award-winning singer-pianist Diana Krall has become a crossover phenomenon – the top-selling jazz vocalist with mass appeal. From Consort, Alberta, k. d. lang has won numerous awards for her songs, and Winnipeg spawned rockers such as Neil Young, and Burton Cummings of The Guess Who ("American Woman").

In the world of opera, Prince Albert, Saskatchewan was home to one of the great tenors of the Wagnerian repertoire, Jon Vickers, who recorded with Herbert von Karajan and sang in many of the world's great opera houses.

Founded in 1939, the Royal Winnipeg Ballet, Canada's oldest professional ballet company, was internationally acclaimed with artistic director Arnold Spohr and dancers such as Evelyn Hart and David Peregrine.

Film and Literature

Western Canada's top film director, Atom Egoyan, won two Academy awards in 1998 for *The Sweet Hereafter*. More recent movies include *Felicia's Journey* and *Ararat*.

Well-known writers include W. O. Mitchell who wrote the Prairie classic, *Who Has Seen the Wind*. Renowned BC artist Emily Carr turned later to writing and produced a unique take on the First Peoples in *Klee Wyck*. Although not a westerner by birth, Archie Belaney (Grey Owl) wrote wonderful nature books such as *Pilgrims of the Wild*, *The Adventures of Sajo and her Beaver People*, and *Tales of an Empty Cabin*.

The evocative poems of Robert Service (*The Shooting of Dan McGrew* and many others) made him almost the national poet of Yukon (see quote, ▶ 80). Born in Yukon in 1920, historian, journalist and media personality Pierre Berton wrote a number of books, including a classic of the Gold Rush (*Klondike*), and two volumes about the construction of the Canadian Pacific Railway (*The National Dream*, *The Last Spike*), serialized for TV, which are required reading before taking the train across Canada.

Science

In the world of science, the internationally respected geneticist David Suzuki, from Vancouver, has consistently received acclaim for his broadcasts explaining the complexities of science in a compelling and lucid way.

Top Ten

Above: *the quintessential image of Western Canada – a forest-ringed lake backed by the snowy peaks of the Rockies*

1
Banff National Park

www.pc.gc.ca/pn-np/ab/banff

29 C2

Visitor Centre and
National Park Office

224 Banff Avenue,
Banff, BC

403/762-1550

Daily 8–8, mid-Jun to
mid-Sep; 8–6, mid-May
to mid-Jun and mid-Sep
to late Sep; 9–5 rest of
year

Canada's oldest national park is arguably its most beautiful, with its sublime scenery, emerald lakes and majestic snow–covered mountains.

Banff National Park was created in the mid-1880s to protect and preserve the hot springs discovered gushing from Sulphur Mountain during construction of the Canadian Pacific Railway. Within its boundaries are the renowned mountain resorts of Banff and Lake Louise, two scenic highways, mighty forests and countless magnificent viewpoints and waterfalls.

Most visitors use Banff Townsite (➤ 40) as a base for exploring the park. From here it's 60km (37 miles) northwest to Lake Louise (➤ 44), following the

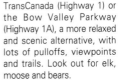

TransCanada (Highway 1) or the Bow Valley Parkway (Highway 1A), a more relaxed and scenic alternative, with lots of pulloffs, viewpoints and trails. Look out for elk, moose and bears.

A highlight on Bow Valley Parkway is Johnston Canyon, 32km (20 miles) west of Banff, which can be seen on the Jonhston Canyon Trail (2km/1.2 miles each way). Here you can walk to two pretty waterfalls.

From Lake Louise, Highway 1 heads west into Yoho National Park (➤ 46), while the scenic Icefields Parkway (➤ 19), one of the world's greatest drives, runs north to Jasper (➤ 42) in Jasper National Park (➤ 20).

The park's lakes are justly famous, and 13km (8 miles) east of Lake Louise is Moraine Lake (➤ 44), a beautiful spot at the foot of the Wenkchemna Mountains.

There are plenty of oppor-

It is possible to find solitude, even in the most popular tourist spots

tunities year-round to pursue outdoor activities – guided hikes, river-rafting, kayaking and golf in summer; downhill and Nordic skiing, tobogganing, snowmobiling and sleigh rides in winter.

2
Butchart Gardens

These stunning gardens, planted with rare and exotic species, are possibly the most spectacular floral display on the continent.

In 1904, Jenny Butchart, the wife of Robert Pim Butchart, a pioneer in the manufacture of Portland cement in Canada, began to develop and landscape the abandoned area created by a worked out quarry from his business. The result is one of the loveliest gardens imaginable and an unmissable stop. The 55-ha (136-acre) gardens lie 22km (13.5 miles) north of Central Victoria, in Brentwood Bay, and contain more than a million individual plants, trees and shrubs representing some 700 different species, collected from around the world.

www.butchartgardens.com

✚ 50 B1

✉ 800 Benvenuto Avenue, Brentwood Bay, Vancouver Island, BC

☎ 866/652-4422, 250/652-5256 (recorded information)

🕐 Daily 9am–10.30pm, midsummer; 9am–sunset, rest of year

🍴 Coffee Bar ($), Blue Poppy Restaurant ($–$$), Dining Room ($$$)

♿ Good

✋ Expensive

The transformation of an industrial blot on the landscape has created one of Canada's most beautiful gardens

Jenny's earliest work, the Sunken Gardens, are set 25m (82ft) below ground level on the floor of the original quarry and are filled with a magnificent collection of flowers, shrubs and classical statuary. The Rose Garden, planted with hybrid tea roses around a wishing well, is best visited in July and August when the air is heavy with the scent of the blooms. Next comes the Japanese Garden, with its rare Himalayan blue poppies, laid out in 1906 with the help of a Japanese landscape gardener. Last is the Italian Garden, the most formal of them all, on the site of the Butcharts' tennis court.

There's something to see at any time of year – including fall foliage and winter berries. It can get very busy at times and you are almost forced along, as if on a conveyor belt. Late afternoons are generally the best time of day to visit, when most of the tour buses have left. The excellent gift store sells a range of seeds, plants and garden accessories, along with excellent First Nations crafts and souvenirs.

3
Howe Sound

www.squamishchamber.bc.ca

50 B1

Squamish Visitor
Information Service
37950 Cleveland Avenue,
Squamish, BC
604/892-9244

**West Coast Railway Heritage
Park**

Squamish, BC

604/898-9336

Daily 10–5

Moderate

www.bcmuseumofmining.org
BC Museum of Mining

Britannia Beach, BC

604/896-2233

Daily 9–4.30. Closed
weekends mid-Oct to
early May

Expensive

*Driving the Sea to Sky
Highway on Howe Sound*

*The drive from Vancouver along the Sea to Sky
Highway reveals awe-inspiring views of
unspoiled scenery.*

The beautiful, fjord-like coastline of Howe Sound was
formed by water erosion, volcanic activity and receding
glaciers. To reach it from Vancouver, head across the
North Shore of Burrard Inlet and go west on Route 1. This
links with the Sea to Sky Highway (Route 99), a
spectacular drive along the twisting shores of the Sound,
past bays and coves, snow-capped peaks and alpine lakes
encircled by firs, on its way to Whistler (▶ 46). As an alternative to driving you can take a leisurely cruise.

It's no longer possible to take the railroad along the
coast, but you can visit the **West Coast Railway Heritage
Park** in Squamish, at the head of Howe Sound, a must-see
for train enthusiasts. Squamish (it's name means "Mother
of the Wind" in the Coast Salish language) is not a particularly attractive town, but it offers a wide range of outdoor
activities including mountaineering, watersports,
horseback riding and spelunking.

The **British Columbia Museum of Mining** at Britannia
Beach is a popular attraction. The copper mine was established in 1899 and in its heyday in the 1920s and 1930s
was the most productive in the British Empire. It closed in
1974 and reopened the following year as this museum,
with mine tours, an interpretive center and a fascinating
account of the mine's history.

4
Icefields Parkway

This 230-km (143-mile) route between Lake Louise and Jasper is one of the world's most spectacular mountain highways.

Officially Route 93, the Icefields Parkway runs through the heart of Banff and Jasper national parks (► 16 and 20), offering endless vistas of snow-capped mountains, interspersed with shimmering lakes, waterfalls and rivers, and the icefields (glaciers) after which it is named.

The whole length of the parkway is a never-ending series of sublime views, but there are some highlights to look out for. Along the first stretch from Lake Louise to Bow Summit are Hector Lake, the second largest lake in Banff National Park, and Crowfoot Glacier, the first of a series of superb glaciers. Bow Lake has one of the best lake walks, the Bow Lake and Bow Glacier Falls Trail, and there are stunning panoramas from Peyto Lake Lookout. Mistaya Canyon is an excellent example of a landscape eroded by the action of water.

Saskatchewan River Crossing, just north of Bow Summit, is the last place to fill up with gas before Jasper. You'll also find refreshments and accommodations here, or you can take the David Thompson Highway east to the small town of Rocky Mountain House, a good place for an overnight stop.

Continuing north, you come to the famous Columbia Icefields, the largest sub-polar sheet of ice and snow in North America, covering around 324sq km (125sq miles) and an estimated 305m (1,000ft) in depth. It sits on the continental divide and its meltwater flows into the Arctic, Pacific and Atlantic oceans. From the Columbia Icefields Centre specially designed "Snocoaches" take you to the middle of the Athabasca Glacier, where you can step out onto the ice. Don't be tempted to go out on your own; hidden cliffs and holes covered by a thin layer of snow are common and deadly hazards.

Dramatic scenery of the Icefields Parkway

Two more highlights stand out before reaching Jasper: the Sunwapta Falls, and the Athabasca Falls (the most photogenic of the two), respectively 56 and 29km (35 and 18 miles) from Jasper.

29 B2

Columbia Icefields Centre

Icefields Parkway, Jasper, Alberta

877/852-6288

Daily 9–5 or 6, May to mid-Oct

5
Jasper National Park

www.
pc.gc.ca/pn-np/ab/jasper

www.
jaspercanadianrockies.com

🗺 29 B2

ℹ Jasper National Park
Information Centre

✉ 500 Connaught Drive,
Jasper, Alberta

☎ 780/852-6176

🕐 Daily 9–7, mid-Jun to
Labour Day; 9–6, Labour
Day–end Sep; 9–5, Apr
to mid-Jun and Oct;
9–5, rest of year

🖐 Park permits: moderate

The natural beauty, wildlife and outdoors activities of Canada's largest national park should tempt you to linger and explore.

Jasper National Park covers an area of 10,880sq km (4,200sq miles), greater than the three other Canadian Rockies' parks combined. Jasper Townsite (➤ 42) is the perfect base for visiting the park, and its visitor center opposite the train station gives an excellent introduction.

The 48-km (30-mile) Maligne Lake Road is the most popular excursion and a good place to spot elk, deer, bighorn sheep, coyote and black bears, especially early or late in the day. It passes Maligne Canyon, up to 55m (180ft) deep and the most spectacular of the accessible canyons in the Rockies. An easy trail loops down part of the canyon from the parking area, taking you past several waterfalls. Medicine Lake, 14km (8.5 miles) farther, is unusual for the fluctuations in its water level; sometimes the lake "disappears" due to an underground drainage system. At the end of the road is Maligne Lake, the largest and most beautiful lake in the Rockies (➤ 24).

Miette Hot Springs, northeast of Jasper Townsite, are the hottest springs in the Canadian Rockies, emerging at a temperature of 54°C (129°F), but they are cooled to a more comfortable 40°C (104°F) as they enter the pool complex.

Running through the heart of the park, from Lake Louise in adjoining Banff National Park, is the Icefields Parkway (➤ 19).

Stunning vistas encircle beautiful Maligne Lake

6
Manitoba Museum of Man and Nature

Winnipeg's spectacular heritage center explores humankind's complex relationship with the natural environment.

www.manitobamuseum.ca

✚ 61 F1

✉ 190 Rupert Avenue, Winnipeg, Manitoba

☎ 204/934-3139, 956-2830 (recorded information)

🕐 Daily 10–5, mid-May to early Sep; Tue–Fri 10–4, Sat–Sun 10–5, rest of year

♿ Good

✋ Moderate

The Centennial Centre (▶ 62) is home to the superb Manitoba Museum of Man and Nature, which opened in 1974 to commemorate the city's centennial. A series of interpretive galleries allows you to experience the sights and sounds of Manitoba, from its earliest known history to the present day.

Begin in the Orientation Gallery, where a wonderful life-size diorama of stampeding bison sets the scene for the theme of the museum. The Earth History Gallery examines Manitoba's geology, from the tropical fossils found in the earth to marine skeletons from 800 million years ago. In the Sub-Arctic Gallery a diorama highlights the life of the northern Inuit, who live by hunting caribou. Look for the polar bears. The Boreal Forest Gallery re-creates the landscape that covers almost a third of the province, and shows moose grazing the tall grasses among the coniferous vegetation.

Not to be missed is the Nonsuch Gallery. It celebrates the coming of Europeans with a life-size re-creation of the two-masted ketch *Nonsuch*, which sailed into Hudson's Bay in 1668 to found the fur trade in Canada. This replica was built in England in 1970 to commemorate the 300th anniversary of the Hudson's Bay Company. You can board the ship in the replicated 17th-century Thames River port, then experience the lifestyle of the fur traders in the Hudson's Bay Company Gallery next door.

The Grasslands Gallery looks at the effect European settlers had on the prairies, while the Urban Gallery traces the rise of Winnipeg and its role in the westward expansion of the pioneers. Pride of place here goes to the bustling 1920s-style street, complete with stores, railroad, theater and movie house. You'll find more than 100 hands-on exhibits in the popular Science Gallery, including the newest exhibit, Water World, and in the Planetarium you can explore the night sky and take a virtual journey to the stars.

Below: *dioramas include this representation of cave painting in progress*
Bottom: *a replica of the ketch,* Nonsuch, *a symbol of early maritime trade*

7

Museum of Anthropology, Vancouver

www.moa.ubc.ca

✚ 50 B1

✉ 6393 Northwest Marine Drive, University of British Columbia Campus, Vancouver, BC

☎ 604/822-5087

🕐 Daily 10–5 (also Tue 5–9), mid-May to Aug; Tue–Sun 11–5 (also Tue 5–9), rest of year

🍴 Café ($)

♿ Excellent

✋ Moderate

Vancouver's finest museum is a superb showcase dedicated to the culture of the local Haida, Salish, Tsimshian and Kwaiutt First Nations.

This museum was the first to treat the lifestyle and art of the native people with the same respect as that of European history, a move that has since been adopted throughout Canada. Arthur Erkickson designed the building in 1976, and his inspiration was the traditional post-and-beam wooden dwellings of the Kwakwaka'wakw people. It is one of the finest examples of modern architecture, whose breathtaking glass-walled, top-lit Great Hall makes a perfect setting for the unrivaled collection of totem poles. Through the large glass windows you can look out on to more totems in the gardens, beautifully framed by the waters of the Georgia Strait.

Alongside the Great Gallery is the Masterpiece Gallery, where you will find a fine collection of intricately carved works in silver, gold, argillite, bone and wood, along with ceremonial masks.

Above: *Bill Reid's magnificent* The Raven and the First Men *is a fine example of the First Nations carving exhibited at the museum*

Right: *the Great Hall has a magnificent display of totems and other First Nations carvings*

Perhaps the museum's single greatest exhibit is the acclaimed cedar sculpture *The Raven and the First Men* in the Rotunda, by world-renowned Haida artist Bill Reid (1920–98). Weighing more than 4 tonnes, it is dominated by a raven sitting on top of a clamshell, while human figures try to escape from it.

The Visible Storage contains many of the museum's artifacts in space-saving, pullout drawers. It's not ideal, but it does mean that you get to see more of the

exhibits that would otherwise be stored away out of sight. Also on site are two traditional longhouses, overlooking Point Gray, built using authentic Haida methods and aligned on the traditional north–south axis.

While you are here, turn right out of the museum for a short walk to the small Nitobe Memorial Garden (open daily; inexpensive), considered the most authentic Japanese garden outside Japan.

Above: *Inuit crafts on display at the museum*

Above: *Part of a totem pole on display in the Great Hall*

8
Rocky Mountains Lakes

29 B2

Information for the lakes may be found on pages cross-referenced within text; otherwise visit **www**.pc.gc.ca for full details of Canada's national and provincial parks

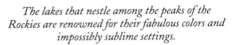

The lakes that nestle among the peaks of the Rockies are renowned for their fabulous colors and impossibly sublime settings.

Many of the lakes owe their intense color to the presence of superfine particles of glacial silt, known as rock flour. When this is suspended in the water it absorbs all incoming light except for the turquoise-blue spectrum. The varying amount in each lake accounts for the wide difference in color, which also changes during the year. In spring there is little rock flour in the water so they are much the same color as other lakes, but as glacial material flows into them during the summer melt, they take on their individual hues once again.

Peyto Lake Lookout has one of the best vistas in the Canadian Rockies

Lake Louise (▶ 44) in Banff National Park is a peerless, sapphire lake, backed by mountains, glaciers and tumbling forests. For fantastic views take the Lake Louise Gondola that runs up Mount Whitehorn, just east of Lake Louise Village.

Just 13km (8 miles) south of Lake Louise is **Moraine Lake** (▶ 44). Much smaller, its water is a deeper blue, and the stupendous snow-dusted Wenckchemna Mountains create a more spectacular backdrop. Stroll along the lakeshore or take the short walk to Consolation Lake.

Maligne Lake in Jasper National Park (▶ 20), the largest lake in the Rockies and the second deepest after **Upper Waterton Lake** (▶ 45), is a wonderful ensemble of water, forest and mountain. Most visitors drive or take a tour along the road, then join one of the 90-minute boat trips on the lake.

Beautiful **Emerald Lake** is one of the quieter spots in the Rockies. It's easily accessed from Field, which lies at the heart of Yoho National Park (▶ 46).

Peyto Lake Lookout in Banff National Park is a highlight of the Icefields Parkway (▶ 19), and has one of the most impressive panoramas in the Rockies, overlooking turquoise Peyto Lake, which nestles at the base of the surrounding mountains.

9
Royal Tyrrell Museum, Drumheller

A highlight of the Alberta Badlands and devoted entirely to dinosaurs, this museum offers an incredible experience for all ages.

The Tyrrell is one of the finest museums of its kind, located about 6km (4.5 miles) northwest of Drumheller, so-called "dinosaur capital of the world" (▶ 76). It takes its name from Joseph Tyrrell, who accidentally stumbled across the bones of an *Albertosaurus* amid the scrub and sagebrush of the Badlands in 1884. This was the first of several hundred complete dinosaur skeletons that have since been excavated, and more are unearthed just about every year.

The museum exhibits around 35 of them, more than any other museum, all strikingly presented in replicated natural surroundings, including the original *Albertosaurus*. *Tyrannosaurus rex* is a predictable favorite, along with more unusual dinosaurs, such as *Xiphactinus*, and *Quetzalcoatlus*, believed to be the largest flying creature ever to have existed. The paleontology collection covers 3.9 billion years and includes some dramatic specimens from the Mesozoic Era.

Computers and videos bring prehistory to life, and other attractions include state-of-the-art displays on the evolution of life on earth, and a primeval garden that reproduces the indigenous vegetation of 350 million years ago. You can also watch scientists at work on fossils in the on-site laboratories, and learn more about Yoho National Park's Burgess Shale fossil beds (▶ 46).

A visit to the museum is best taken in conjunction with a trip to the Dinosaur Provincial Park (▶ 76), where you will find one of the museum's field stations.

www.tyrrellmuseum.com

 60 B2

 Highway 838, Midland Provincial Park, Drumheller, Alberta

 403/823-7707, 888/440-4240 (toll free in North America)

 Daily 9–9, mid-May to early Sep; Tue–Sun 10–5, rest of year

 Cafeteria ($)

 Good

 Moderate

More than 35 dinosaur skeletons are on show

10
Stanley Park, Vancouver

www.city.vancouver.bc.ca

50 B1

Western tip of downtown Vancouver, BC

604/257-8400

Freely accessible

Cafés along the seawall at Prospect Point and Ferguson Point

Walkways in sculpted area fully accessible

Free

Below: *a totem in the park*
Bottom: *close encounters with belugas are part of the aquarium experience*

You can't come to Vancouver and not visit Stanley Park, one of the world's greatest urban parks, and an oasis close to the heart of downtown.

Stanley Park was set aside as permanent public parkland in 1888 when the British Government handed its 405ha (1,000 acres) over to the city. This semi-wilderness of dense rain forest, woodland glades and marshland juts out into Burrard Inlet, with water on three sides. On the park's eastern fringe are the more manicured gardens and a medley of sights and self-contained attractions, including the Lost Lagoon, a shallow tidal haven for a host of birds such as cormorants, mergansers and scaup; the 5,000-bush Rose Garden; and the state-of-the-art Vancouver Aquarium (▶ 34).

A horse-drawn bus is great for getting an overview of Stanley Park, but the best way to really appreciate what's on offer is to walk, cycle or roller-blade the 16-km (10-mile) Sea Wall that circles the park. Even if you don't do the whole circuit you should enjoy the superlative views from some part of it. Prospect Point, perched on a cliff at the northern tip of the park, is the highest point, and from here you can see the North Shore (▶ 33), and out into the Pacific beyond English Bay. The sandy beaches come as a real surprise, being so close to the downtown area of this huge metropolis.

The park has plenty of activities that are suitable for all ages, including the Children's Farmyard, a miniature railroad, a water park, a heated oceanside swimming pool and the Theatre under the Stars.

What To See

CARIBOO
GOLD RUSH TRAIL

Above: *glittering reflections of Vancouver*
Right: *gold still brings visitors to the West*

British Columbia & The Rockies

The Pacific province of British Columbia, Canada's third largest, is a land of extensive plateaus, myriad lakes, great rivers caught between rugged mountains, and islands lying off its much-indented coastline. Its natural splendor allows for a wealth of outdoor activities, from climbing, hiking and skiing to sailing, canoeing and fishing. Touring by bus, car or RV is easy and the roads are excellent.

When BC became part of Canada in 1871, about a quarter of the inhabitants were First Nations people. British settlers were followed by large groups of Chinese laborers who came to work in the gold mines and on the railroad. Today many Far Eastern influences add to the province's multicultural mix.

BC is separated from the rest of Canada by the Rocky Mountains, a natural barrier that it shares with Alberta. Access across this mighty patchwork of dramatic peaks, pristine forests and emerald lakes is via three mountain passes – Crowsnest, Kicking Horse and Yellowhead.

'British Columbia… If I had known what it was like, I wouldn't have been content with a mere visit. I'd have been born here.'

STEPHEN LEACOCK
Canadian humorist (1937)

BRITISH COLUMBIA & THE ROCKIES

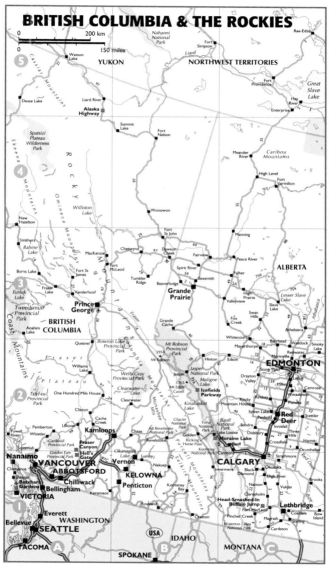

0   200 km
0   150 miles

YUKON

NORTHWEST TERRITORIES

Rae-Edzo

Nahanni
National
Park

Fort
Simpson

Liard
River

Fort
Providence

Great
Slave
Lake

Watson
Lake

Hay
River

Enterprise

Deese Lake

Liard River

**Alaska
Highway**

Summit
Lake

Fort
Nelson

Meander
River

Caribou
Mountains

Spatsizi
Plateau
Wilderness
Park

High Level

Fort
Vermilion

New
Hazelton

Williston
Lake

Wonowon

Smithers

Babine
Lake

Fort St
John

Manning

Dawson
Creek

Fairview

Peace River

Fox
Creek

ALBERTA

Burns Lake

Fraser
Lake

Fort St
James

MacKenzie

Chetwynd

Fort
McLeod

Spirit River

Beaverlodge

Fahler

High
Prairie

Lesser Slave
Lake

Eutsuk
Lake

Tumbler
Ridge

Smoky

Grande Prairie

Sexsmith

Valleyview

Swan
Hills

Slave
Lake

**Tweedsmuir
Provincial
Park**

Vanderhoof

**Prince
George**

Grande
Cache

Athabasca

Anahim
Lake

**BRITISH
COLUMBIA**

Quesnel

Bowron Lake
Provincial
Park

Whitecourt

Barrhead

Westlock

Redwater

Smoky
Lake

Mt Robson
Provincial
Park

Mayerthorpe

EDMONTON

Williams
Lake

Mt Robson
3954

Hinton

Edson

Marinville

Drayton
Valley

Wells Gray
Provincial
Park

Jasper
National
Park

Jasper

Mt Edith
Cavell
3363

Rimbey

Camrose

Wetaskiwin

One Hundred Mile House

Clearwater
Lake

Clearwater

Maligne
Lake

**Icefields
Parkway**

Kinbasket
Lake

Rocky
Mountain House

Sylvan Lake

Penhold

**Red
Deer**

Stettler

Tsyl-os
Provincial
Park

Clinton

Cache
Creek

Chase

Glacier
National
Park

Mt Revelstoke
National Park

Yoho
National
Park

Lake Louise

Banff
National
Park

Sundre

Didsbury

Innisfail

Three
Hills

Hanna

Powell
River

Pemberton

Lillooet

Whistler

Kamloops

Revelstoke

Golden

Kicking
Horse Pass

Moraine Lake

Banff

Crossfield

Strathmore

Drumheller

Squamish

Garibaldi
Provincial Park

**Fraser
Canyon**

**Hell's
Gate**

Lumby

Okanagan
Lake

Nakusp

Kootenay
National Park

Canmore

CALGARY

Okotoks

Brooks

Nanaimo

Golden Ears
Provincial Park

VANCOUVER

ABBOTSFORD

Vernon

Invermere

Black
Diamond

High River

Vulcan

Chilliwack

KELOWNA

Kootenay
Bay

Nanton

Cochrane

Cowichan

Butchart
Gardens

Bellingham

Keremeos

Penticton

Rossland

Creston

**Head-Smashed-In
Buffalo Jump**

Fort Macleod

Claresholm

Coaldale

Lethbridge

VICTORIA

Bellevue

Everett

WASHINGTON

Pincher Creek

Waterton Lakes
National Park

Magrath

Sterling

Bow
Island

SEATTLE

IDAHO

Cardston

TACOMA

SPOKANE

MONTANA

USA

⑤ ④ ③ ② ①

A   B   C

Vancouver

Its dazzling setting alone – ringed by the waters of the Pacific and the majestic snow-capped peaks of the Coast Mountains – makes Vancouver a must on any visit to British Columbia.

www.tourism-vancouver.org

29 A1

200 Burrard Street

604/683-2000

Daily 8–6, Jun–Aug;
Mon–Fri 8.30–5, Sat 9–5,
rest of year

Vancouver has a stunning waterfront location

Few cities can match Canada's Gateway to the Pacific. Its busy multicultural population lends the city a cosmopolitan air, and together with great shopping and wonderful restaurants, outstanding museums and galleries, a vast range of recreational activities, a buzzing nightlife, green parks and fabulous views, you'll be hard pressed to know where to start.

Canada Place makes a stunning introduction to Vancouver, with sensational views of the city's port. Downtown occupies a wonderful natural setting on the

Little wonder Vancouver features on countless cruise-ship itineraries

south shore of Burrard Inlet with the Strait of Georgia just offshore; its attractions cover a small area and are easily walkable. Granville Island, with its fabulous market, really buzzes, especially on weekends, and Chinatown bursts with sights, sounds and smells, while Gastown, the redeveloped heart of Vancouver, is a dynamic mix of stores, bars and restaurants. Commercial Drive, north

of Broadway, is the city's traditional Little Italy district, and residential North Shore has some of the country's most expensive real estate. And when you need to unwind, Stanley Park is the perfect place to counter the stress that comes with any city visit.

What to See in Vancouver

CANADA PLACE   ✪✪✪

For the best view of Vancouver's port and spectacular natural setting, you can't beat Canada Place. Jutting out into Burrard Inlet, this waterfront building with its five vast "sails" is one of the most distinctive features on the Vancouver skyline. Originally built for Expo '86, it is now home to stores, restaurants, hotels, a convention center and an IMAX theater. A stroll along the promenade comes with sensational views of the city's skyscrapers, surrounding mountains and the cruise ship terminal, where some of the world's most luxurious vessels dock. There is an equally good viewpoint a short walk away at the Harbour Centre Building, where all-glass SkyLifts whisk you up to **The Lookout!**, a circular observation deck.

www.canadaplace.ca
- ✉ 100-999 Canada Place Way
- ☎ 604/775-8687, IMAX theater 604/682-4629
- ⏱ Daily
- 🚌 1 on Burrard, 3, 4, 6, 7, 8, on Granville
- 🚈 Skytrain: Waterfront
- ♿ Good
- 💵 Free; IMAX: expensive

www.vancouverlookout.com
The Lookout!
- ✉ 555 West Hastings Street
- ☎ 604/689-0421
- ⏱ Daily 8.30–10.30, May–Sep; 9–9 rest of year
- 💵 Expensive

31

Along East Pender, Abbot and Keefer streets and Gore Avenue

🚌 19, 22 east on Pender Street

www. discovervancouverchinese garden.com
Dr. Sun-Yat Sen Chinese Garden

✉ 578 Carrall Street
☎ 604/662-3207
🕐 Daily 10–6 or 7, May to mid-Sep; 10–4.30, rest of year
🍴 Café ($)
🚌 19, 22
♿ Moderate

CHINATOWN ✪✪

North America's third-largest Chinatown (after San Francisco and New York) dates from around 1858 when Chinese immigrants flocked here during the Fraser Valley Gold Rush. Many more followed to work on the transcontinental railroad in the 1880s. Today this fascinating district is crammed with tiny, crowded streets and alleys, vibrant markets and stores filled with oriental food and ancient herbal remedies. You can buy almost anything at the night market that takes place on Friday, Saturday and Sunday evenings (6–11pm). Take in some of the exotic stores and restaurants, then visit the **Dr. Sun Yat-Sen Chinese Garden**, named after the founder of the Chinese Republic, who was a regular visitor to Vancouver. A harmonious blend of plantings and space, the gardens were created in classical Chinese style.

> ### DID YOU KNOW?
>
> The 1913 Sam Kee Building, at 8 West Pender Street in Chinatown, is listed in the *Guinness Book of World Records* as the narrowest building in the world. It measures just 2m (6.5ft) wide.

www.granvilleisland.bc.ca
Granville Island Infocentre

✉ 1398 Cartwright Street
☎ 604/666-5784, 604/666-6655

🍴 Many cafés, bars and restaurants ($–$$$)
🚌 50

Food Market
✉ 1689 Johnston Street
☎ 604/666-5784
🕐 Daily 9–6. Closed Mon in winter

Granville Island Brewery
✉ 1441 Cartwright Street
☎ 604/687-2637
🕐 Tours Jun–Sep

Granville Island Museums
✉ 1502 Duranleau Street
☎ 604/683-1939
🕐 Tue–Sun 10–5.30
♿ Moderate

GRANVILLE ISLAND ✪✪✪

Granville Island is one of Vancouver's most vibrant cultural centers. This former swampland has been transformed into an attractive riverside area, following several periods of regeneration. Connected to downtown by the Granville Street Bridge, it is a thriving medley of stores, restaurants, galleries, artists' studios, nightclubs and one of the world's greatest **food markets**, with a stunning array of meat, fish, cheese, fruit, wine and specialty food stands. In addition to the wonderful bustling food market, there's the **Granville Island Brewery**, which offers guided tours and tastings, and a trio of **museums** under one roof featuring sport fishing, model ships and model trains.

Granville Island market is one of the best anywhere

MARITIME MUSEUM ✪✪

Take the water taxi from Granville Island to Vanier Park, where the Maritime Museum explores Vancouver's strong ties with the sea. Pride of place goes to the *St. Roch*, a two-masted Royal Canadian Mounted Police schooner, built in the 1920s. In 1944 it became the first vessel to sail through the treacherous Northwest Passage between Baffin Island and Alaska's Beaufort Sea. There is also a section about pirates – Pirate's Cove – and a Children's Maritime Discovery Centre, with exciting hands-on exhibits and tales of the sea, plus a huge collection of model ships, period photographs and memorabilia.

MUSEUM OF ANTHROPOLOGY (➤ 22–23, TOP TEN)

NORTH SHORE ✪✪

Vancouver's North Shore – comprising the District of West Vancouver and the District and City of North Vancouver – lies across Burrard Inlet and English Bay. It's a recreational paradise, backed by Grouse Mountain, Capilano Regional Park, Lighthouse Park, and the Cypress, Lyn Canyon and Mount Seymour provincial parks, and is particularly popular for hiking and walking in summer and for skiing in winter.

Access to the exclusive residential area of West Vancouver is via the Lion's Gate Bridge at the tip of Stanley Park (➤ 26) and to North Vancouver by SeaBus from the terminal near Canada Place (➤ 31).

Lonsdale Quay in North Vancouver has great shopping, including a fine indoor market, and you can watch the ships come and go in the harbor from the observation tower or nearby Waterfront Park.

Cypress, Grouse and Seymour mountains dominate the scene, but the undoubted highlight is Grouse Mountain. Here you are whisked by cable-car to the top, where the Theatre in the Sky gives incredible panoramic views of Vancouver and its surroundings.

Below Grouse Mountain, Capilano Gorge has the world's oldest (1889) and longest (137m/450ft) suspension footbridge (entrance fee), swaying 76m (250ft) above the rushing waters of the Capilano River.

---

www.vmm.bc.ca
✉ 1095 Ogden Avenue
☎ 604/257-8300
🕐 Daily 10–5. Closed Mon early Sep–Apr
🚌 2, 22 🚤 Water taxi from Granville Island
♿ Good 💰 Moderate

Above: *the* St. Roch, *now in the Maritime Museum, was the first vessel to navigate the Northwest Passage*

---

www.nvchamber.bc.ca
North Shore Tourism
✉ 102–124 West 1st Street, North Vancouver
☎ 604/987-4488
🍴 Range of eateries along North Shore ($–$$$)
🚌 250, 257
🚢 SeaBus to North Vancouver

www.capbridge.com
Capilano Canyon Suspension Bridge
✉ 3735 Capilano Road, North Vancouver
☎ 604/985-7474
🕐 Daily May–Sep
💰 Expensive

www.grousemountain.com
Grouse Mountain Cable Car
✉ 6400 Nancy Greene Way, North Vancouver
☎ 604/984-0661
🕐 Daily 9am–10pm
💰 Expensive

www.scienceworld.bc.ca
- ✉ 1455 Québec Street
- ☎ 604/443-7443 (24-hour information)
- 🕐 Mon–Fri 10–5, Sat–Sun 10–6
- 🍴 White Spot Triple O ($)
- 🚌 3, 8 north on Granville Mall, 19 on Pender Street
- Ⓢ SkyTrain to Science World-Main Street
- 💲 Expensive

Above: *the striking architecture of Science World*

www.vanaqua.org
- ✉ 845 Avison Way, Stanley Park
- ☎ 604/659-3552
- 🕐 Daily 9.30–7, Jul–Aug; 10–5.30, rest of year. Call ahead for feeding times.
- 🍴 Upstream Café ($)
- 🚌 23, 35, 135, 240, 246
- ♿ Good
- 💲 Expensive

SCIENCE WORLD ✪✪

Science World's futuristic geodesic dome at the eastern end of False Creek, built for Expo '86, has become a distinctive Vancouver landmark. Here the mysteries of science are unraveled in a lively and entertaining way, with daily demonstrations at the ground level center stage and hands-on interactive displays. In addition to five permanent galleries – Eureka, the Sara Stern Gallery, KidSpace, Our World and Visual Illusions – there is a Special Exhibitions Gallery and a science theater. The OMNIMAX theater on the upper level shows the latest blockbuster movies on one of the largest dome screens in the world.

STANLEY PARK (▶ 26, TOP TEN)

VANCOUVER AQUARIUM ✪✪✪

Stanley Park (▶ 26) is home to the superb Vancouver Aquarium, which attracts more than a million visitors each year, making it Canada's second-most popular visitor attraction (after Toronto's CN Tower). Inside are more than 8,000 aquatic creatures, representing over 600 different marine species, with the emphasis on those from the Northwest and the Arctic. To get the best from your visit, check the schedule of activities; information is available in the Upper Pacific Canada Pavilion.

It's hard not to be impressed by the re-creations of a humid Amazon rain forest with giant sloths, iguanas, brightly colored tropical birds and crocodiles, and an Indonesian coral reef, complete with angelfish and blacktip reef sharks, but for most people the big draw is undoubtedly the whales. The Arctic Canada habitat gives you the chance to see beluga whales close up through huge underwater windows. Although these graceful creatures are well cared for, there has been concern from animal rights' groups about keeping large sea mammals in captivity. It remains an ongoing issue.

Children enjoy the tidal pools, where they can touch anemones and starfish. Also popular are the delightful antics of the sea otters, sea lions and harbor seals.

VANCOUVER ART GALLERY ✪✪

A former 1911 city courthouse has been transformed into downtown's principal sight, the Vancouver Art Gallery. The highlight is the outstanding collection by British Columbia's best known artist, Emily Carr (1871–1945), containing several of her evocative rain forest scenes. Her haunting paintings capture the brooding power of the Canadian wilderness.

The gallery also features works by Dutch, French, Italian, German and English masters, photography, sculpture, graphics and video works, and presents touring historical and contemporary exhibitions.

The neoclassical building, a work of art in its own right, was redesigned in the 1980s by Arthur Erickson and makes a wonderful setting for the art. The café serves excellent coffee, snacks and light meals and the gallery shop has a fine range of unique handcrafted items.

www.vanartgallery.bc.ca
✉ 750 Hornby Street
☎ 604/662-4719
🕐 Daily 10–5.30 (also Thu 5.30–9). Closed Mon in winter
🍴 Gallery Café ($–$$)
🚌 5, 15 and tourist trolley
🚇 Burrard or Granville
♿ Good
💲 Expensive

Artist George Pepper has a unique take on the British Columbia landscape

VANCOUVER MUSEUM ✪✪

In 1968 Canada's largest civic museum moved to its present location in a futuristic building designed by Gerald Hamilton. Its extensive collections – hundred of thousands of specimens and artifacts – make an excellent job of tracing the history of Vancouver and the First Nations.

The appalling conditions endured by immigrants traveling in "steerage" across the Atlantic from Europe are vividly brought to life, while the Pacific Rim Collection emphasizes western Canada's strong associations with China, Japan and Oceania. Other highlights include an old Hudson's Bay Company outpost and a Canadian Pacific Railway car.

The H. R. MacMillan Planetarium shares the same building. Here, among other things, you can take a virtual trip to Mars or try to design a spacecraft.

www.vanmuseum.bc.ca
✉ 1100 Chestnut Street, Vanier Park
☎ 604/736-4431
🕐 Tue–Sun 10–5 (also Thu 5–9). Closed Dec 25
🍴 Vending machines ($)
♿ Good
🚌 2, 22
💲 Moderate

In the Know

10
Ways To Be A Local

Dress casually, even for dinner – cowboy boots in Calgary, a feed-company cap in Manitoba, a fleece vest north of 60 (degrees latitude, that is).

Call everyone by their first name. "Mister" and "Mrs." are virtually banned west of Lake Superior. Even loan applicants call their bank managers by their first name.

Learn to say First Nations rather than Indians, natives or (worst of all) red Indians. And in the north, they're Inuit not Eskimos. Canada's aboriginal peoples are nowhere more visible than they are in the North and the West.

Go to a Canadian Football League game in the fall and cheer for the local team. NEVER cheer for an eastern team.

Order your coffee double, double (two cream, two sugars; double Twin if you want sugar substitute; "single" for one measure). Never ask for "white" coffee – you won't be understood.

Learn to discuss the finer points of curling (a game played on ice with big lumps of granite) – especially useful in small Prairie towns where the local rink is often the main social center in winter.

Jog around the Sea Wall in Vancouver's Stanley Park alongside the city's fitness fanatics.

Tell Winnipeggers their smoked meat is better than Montréal's.

Spend Saturday night people-watching on Calgary's "Red Mile" (17th Avenue from 4th to 8th streets).

Restrain yourself from saying anything nice about Ottawa or Toronto.

10
Good Places to Have Lunch

Barb's Place ✉ Fisherman's Wharf, Erie Street, Victoria ☎ 250/384-6515. Floating kitchen serves takeout fish and chips, oysters and chowder that you can eat at nearby picnic tables.

Mary's Diner ✉ 1202 Davie Street, Vancouver ☎ 604/687-1293. Huge juicy hamburgers and marvelous meatloaf with garlic mashed potatoes.

Tony's Fish & Oyster Café ✉ 1511 Anderson Street, Vancouver ☎ 604/683-7127. Granville

Chairlift and mountain views at Whistler

Island landmark serves fresh oysters, and huge seafood platters that are ideal for sharing.

Bullock's Bistro ✉ 4 Lessard Dive, Yellowknife ☎ 867/873-3474. Tiny place, tiny menu – but hard to beat the pan-fried fish.

Buzzards Cowboy Cuisine ✉ 140 10th Avenue SW, Calgary ☎ 403/264-6959. Features such traditional Western delicacies as slow roasted barbecued pulled beef on a bun.

Da-De-O ✉ 10548A 82nd Avenue, Edmonton ☎ 780/433-0930. 1950s-style diner that serves up Cajun favorites like po-boy sandwiches and blackened catfish.

Bushwakker Brewing Co Ltd ✉ 2206 Dewdney Avenue, Regina ☎ 306/359-7276. Big, breezy brewpub serves gourmet pizzas and steaks.

Wanuskewin Restaurant ✉ Wanuskewin Heritage Park, Saskatoon ☎ 306/931-6767. Lunch on bison steak, wild rice and bannock in a room overlooking the beautiful Opimihaw Valley.

Alycia's ✉ 559 Cathedral Avenue, Winnipeg ☎ 204/582-8789. Menu reflects the West's Ukrainian heritage – *pirogis*, cabbage rolls and *kolbassa* sausages.

Bistro Dansk ✉ 63 Sherbrook Street, Winnipeg ☎ 204/775-5662. Danish open-face sandwiches in a cozy setting.

Canoeing on Lake Louise – perfect peace

10 Top Activities

- **Skiing** Alberta and British Columbia resorts are among the world's best.
- **Horseback riding** Dude ranches and trail riding dot the West and Yukon.
- **Hiking** Especially in Banff and Jasper national parks.
- **Whitewater rafting** Most challenging runs are in northern BC and Yukon.
- **Sailing** off the BC coast and on Great Slave Lake.
- **Salmon fishing** Permits required.
- **Climbing** in the Rockies.
- **Whale-watching**
- **Golf**
- **Birding and wildlife watching**

5 Best Parks

Banff (Alberta, ➤ 40)
Pacific Rim (BC, ➤ 56)
Gwaii Haanas (BC, ➤ 57)
Kluane (Yukon, ➤ 88)
Cypress Hills (Saskatchewan, ➤ 74, 75)

5 Unusual Activities

Midnight rides (Yukon)
Kayaking among orcas (BC)
Polar bear watching (Manitoba)
Glacier skiing (Alberta)
Gold panning (Yukon)

Downtown Vancouver

Distance
3.2 km (2 miles)

Time
2 hours (not including tours and shopping)

Start point
Canada Place

End point
Aquabus terminal Hornby Street

Lunch
Yaletown Brewing Company ($$)
 1111 Mainland
☎ 604/681-2739

This walk across downtown includes main shopping streets (Burrard and Robson), the cathedral and art gallery.

Start at Canada Place (➤ 31).

The impressive cruise ship terminus offers majestic views north across the waters of Burrard Inlet and Coal Harbour.

Walk away from the waterfront on Burrard Street to the 19th-century, neo–Gothic Christ Church Cathedral.

The cathedral sits on the corner of Burrard and West Georgia. Turn left here, stopping to admire the fine exterior of Hotel Vancouver on the opposite corner.

Walk half a block along West Georgia to Hornby Street. Check out the pendulum in the lobby of the HSBC Bank directly ahead. Cross Georgia and take Hornby Street.

The Vancouver Art Gallery (➤ 35), occupies the prize downtown real estate to your left.

Where Robson Street intersects Hornby turn left and continue past the Pacific Shopping Mall.

After five blocks you'll see the unmistakable façade of the Public Library ahead on the corner of Robson and Homer. With its curves and colonnaded outer façade, it resembles the Colosseum of ancient Rome.

Turn right on Homer Street.

Look out for the BC Place Stadium, which comes into view left down intersecting streets as you stroll.

Pass the Chintz and Company store on the left, then turn left on Nelson Street into Yaletown.

This rundown warehouse district was transformed in the 1990s into the trendiest area of the downtown peninsula.

Head to the corner of Hamilton and Davie streets and go right. Walk uphill to rejoin Hornby Street. Turn left to the waterfront for the Aquabus to Granville Island (➤ 32).

Robson Street, the hub of Vancouver's upscale shopping, blends many architectural styles

What to See in British Columbia and the Rockies

ALASKA HIGHWAY ⭐⭐⭐

One of the world's great adventures, the Alaska Highway recalls the intrepid journeys of old in North America's northern frontiers. Today's highway is a far cry from the original route that was laid out through mosquito-infested swampland in 1942 as a military access road. It ran for 2,446km (1,520 miles), winding its way from Dawson Creek in British Columbia to Fairbanks in Alaska (USA). Although it officially ends at Delta Junction, most people continue to Fairbanks, 158km (98 miles) farther.

Also known as the Alcan Highway, it begins as Highway 97 in Dawson Creek, traditionally at the Mile Zero cairn. Fort St. John (Mile 47) is the oldest European settlement on mainland British Columbia and Stone Mountain Provincial Park (Mile 392) has the highest point on the road at Summit Lake (1,378m/4,521ft). Laird Hot Springs (Mile 496) rank among the finest natural hot springs in Canada. The pools here have an average temperature of 46°C (115°F) and are surrounded by a lush floral carpet, including many species of orchid.

From here it's another 224km (139 miles) to Watson Lake (Mile 635), the Yukon's first town (▶ 85). The highway crosses the Yukon border several times between Mile 588 and 627, the official crossing. At Watson Lake the Campbell Highway swings north and west and runs parallel to the Alaska Highway through eastern Yukon, ending at Carmacks.

The highway is accessible year round, weather permitting. If you plan to drive the whole route, remember it involves crossing the US border, so take the necessary documents and currency.

➕ 29 A5

ℹ️ Dawson Creek Visitor Information Centre

✉️ Station Museum

☎️ 250/782-9595

ℹ️ Fort St. John Visitor Information Centre

✉️ 9523 - 100th Street, Fort St. John, BC

☎️ 250/785-3033

Above: *The Alaska Highway was constructed in a hurry during World War II as a supply route to northwest coastal defenses*

DID YOU KNOW?

The straightening of the Alaska Highway's notorious curves means that it is now only 2,395km (1,488 miles) from Dawson Creek (Mile Zero) to the old Mile 1520 marker post at Fairbanks.

---

www.pc.gc.ca/pn-np/ab/banff

🔲 29 C2

ℹ️ Banff Information Centre

✉️ 224 Banff Avenue, Banff

☎️ 403/762-1550

🕐 Daily 8–6, mid-May to late
Sep (to 8 peak season);
9–5, rest of year

**Whyte Museum of the
Canadian Rockies**

✉️ 111 Bear Street, Banff

☎️ 403/762-2291

🕐 Daily 10–5 💰 Moderate

**Cave and Basin National
Historic Site**

✉️ 311 Cave Avenue

☎️ 403/762-1566

🕐 Daily 9–6 mid-May to Sep;
Mon–Fri 9.30–5, Sat–Sun
11–4 rest of year.

💰 Inexpensive

Banff Upper Hot Springs

www.pc.gc.ca/pn-np/ab/banff

✉️ Mountain Avenue, Banff,
Alberta

☎️ 403/726-1515

🕐 Daily 9am–11pm mid-May
to late Oct; 10–10 (also
10–11pm Fri–Sat), rest of
year 💰 Moderate

*The Sulphur Mountain
Gondola provides access
to wonderful vistas*

🔲 29 A1

ℹ️ Quesnel Chamber of
Commerce

✉️ 705 Carson Street,
Quesnel

☎️ 205/992-8716

www.barkerville.ca

Barkerville Historic Town

✉️ PO Box 19, Barkerville,

☎️ 250/994-3302

🕐 Daily late May–Sep

💰 Moderate

BANFF

Banff's superb location – at 1,383m (4,537ft), it's the highest town in Canada – its excellent visitor center and its attractions make it an obvious base for exploring Banff National Park (► 16). The **Whyte Museum of the Canadian Rockies**, portraying local life and landscapes with paintings, photographs and artifacts, is worth a visit.

The **Sulphur Mountain Gondola**, 3.2km (2 miles) south of town on Mountain Avenue, provides a daily cable-car ride (expensive) up to Canada's highest restaurant for fine views, while the **Cave and Basin National Historic Site**, to the southeast, is an interpretive center based

around the hot springs discovered here in 1883. If you want to take a dip and unwind, you'll need to head instead for **Upper Hot Springs**, a modern complex where the sulfurous waters emerge at a steamy 42°C (108°F).

BANFF NATIONAL PARK (► 16, TOP TEN)

CARIBOO CHILCOTIN

This vast range stretches from the fjords of the Pacific Coast across British Columbia's interior plateau to the foothills of the Cariboo Mountains. It's gold country, it's cattle country, it's vast forests and it has a deeply indented coastline, small fishing villages and coastal rain forests. It has some of the world's largest cattle ranches and much of BC's best freshwater fishing. Bella Coola, a sport fisherman's dream, is located where the Bella Coola River joins the Pacific, at the end of the 459-km (285-mile) Highway 20 from Williams Lake. The Cariboo Highway, from Williams Lake to Quesnel, is the heart of the area.

Quesnel, north of Williams Lake, was built in the 1860s at the junction of the Fraser and Quesnel rivers. From here prospectors traveled to the local gold fields. Today tourists follow, to visit the Gold Rush town of **Barkerville**. Following reconstruction of more than 100 buildings, it re-creates all the excitement of those days.

FRASER CANYON AND HELL'S GATE

In 1808 American-born fur trader Simon Fraser led an expedition in birch-bark canoes down what he thought was the Columbia River. It wasn't, and the river now bears his name. Rising in Mount Robson National Park, the mighty Fraser, one of Canada's great waterways, flows 1,279km (795 miles) southwest to the Pacific. About 48km (30 miles) south of Lytton, a staging post on the old Cariboo Road to the goldfields, is Hell's Gate, nature at its most magnificent. Here the Fraser Canyon, 183m (600ft) deep and just 30m (98ft) wide, forces the river into a narrow channel, and at peak spring levels water equaling twice the volume of Niagara Falls surges through here.

The **Hell's Gate AirTram** cable-car descends into the gorge to a suspension bridge and observation deck for great views of the raging river below. In 1913 a landslide occurred during construction of the Canadian Pacific Railway, which wiped out millions of spawning salmon. It wasn't until 1945 that fish ladders were completed to enable them to bypass the gorge.

www.hellsgateairtram.com
➕ 29 A1/2
Hell's Gate AirTram
✉ Hell's Gate, 9.6km (6 miles) north of Yale
☎ 604/867-9277
🕐 Daily, mid-Apr to mid-Oct
🍴 Café ($), Salmon House Restaurant ($–$$)
♿ Moderate

Cave and Basin National Historic Site

GLACIER AND MOUNT REVELSTOKE NATIONAL PARKS ⭐⭐

The mountains immediately to the west of the Rockies are every bit as spectacular as the Rockies themselves, and parts are protected by these two small adjoining national parks.

Glacier National Park, the larger and more easterly of the two, remained virtually uninhabited until the Canadian Pacific Railway was driven through in 1885 via Rogers Pass. Visitors flocked to the pass's hotel, but the line closed in 1916 when the Connaught tunnel opened, and tourist numbers only recovered when the TransCanada Highway opened. Some 14 percent of the park is permanently under snow, and has more than 420 glaciers, while the rest is a feast of stunning scenery. The **Rogers Pass Visitor Centre** has details of walks, and just south of the center Illecillewaet Neve is one of the most impressive glaciers in the park.

To the west, **Mount Revelstoke National Park** was created in 1914 to protect the mountain's alpine meadows. The main access is on the 26-km (16-mile) Meadows in the Sky Parkway, near the town of Revelstoke. The aptly named parkway climbs toward the summit of Mount Revelstoke (1,938m/6,358ft) where there are walks and hikes, and places to enjoy the view or have a picnic.

www.pc.gc.ca/pn-np/bc /revelstoke or /glacier
➕ 29 B2
ℹ Rogers Pass Visitor Centre
☎ 250/837-7500
🕐 Daily 8am–8.30pm, mid-Jun to mid-Sep; 9–5, May to mid-Jun and mid-Sep to Oct; 7–5, Dec–Apr; Thu–Mon 9–5, Nov

HOWE SOUND (▶ 18, TOP TEN)

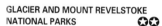

DID YOU KNOW?

Hope, at the entrance to Fraser Canyon, is called the "Chainsaw Carving Capital of Canada." Pete Ryan's fabulous carvings are known worldwide for their beauty and unique style, and they can be viewed by picking up a copy of the Hope Arts and Carving Walk from the Infocentre.

29 B2

Jasper Visitor Information

409 Patricia Street,

780/852-3858

Yellowhead Museum

400 Pyramid Lake Road

780/852-3013

Daily 10–9, mid-May to
early Sep; 10–5, rest of
year. Closed Mon–Wed
mid-Oct to mid-May

Inexpensive

www.jaspertramway.com

Jasper Tramway

Whistler Mountain Road

780/852-3093

Daily 8.30am–10pm,
Jul–Aug; 9.30–6.30, Jun &
Sep; 9.30–4.30, mid-Apr
to May & early to mid-Oct

Moderate

www.
pc.gc.ca/pn-np/bc/kootenay

29 B2

Park Visitor Centre

Radium Hot Springs

250/347-9615, 250/347-
9505

Daily 9–7, late Jun–early
Sep; 9.30–4.30, late
May–late Jun and early
Sep to mid-Sep

Inexpensive

*Desirable real estate on
Kootenay Lake*

ICEFIELDS PARKWAY (► 19, TOP TEN)

JASPER

Jasper is the main town in beautiful rugged Jasper
National Park (► 20), the largest preserved wilderness area
in the Rocky Mountains. It focuses on two main thorough-
fares – Connaught Drive and Patricia Street. The excellent
park visitor center at 500 Connaught Drive is a natural
historic site in an attractive garden setting and a gathering
place for visitors. The main attraction in town is the
Yellowhead Museum and Archives, with modest
displays that highlight the town's history and its role in the
fur trade. It also has a small art gallery.

The **Jasper Tramway**, a cable-car 7km (4.3 miles)
south of town, takes visitors 2,298m (7,867ft) up Whistler
Mountain. It's very busy in summer so arrive early, but it's
worth the wait for the wonderful views. There's also a
restaurant, interpretive center and a trail that continues up
the mountain for even more impressive panoramas.

JASPER NATIONAL PARK (► 20, TOP TEN)

KOOTENAY NATIONAL PARK

Kootenay is the least visited of the four Rocky Mountain
national parks, but it's jagged peaks and river-cut forests
are as impressive as any in Canada. Long and narrow, the
park is bisected by the Banff–Windermere Parkway
(Highway 93), linking all the major attractions. It enters from
the east at Castle Junction. Eight kilometers (5 miles) from
here, on the BC-Alberta border, is Vermilion Pass
(1,651m/5,417ft), marking the Continental Divide, from
where rivers flow west to the Pacific and east to the
Atlantic. About 3km (1.8 miles) south of Vermilion Pass is
the starting point for the Glacier Trail to a superb view of
Stanley Glacier and the Hanging Valley below Stanley Peak.

Marble Canyon, a 37-m (121-ft) deep gorge 8km
(5 miles) south of Vermilion Pass, is the main point of
interest. The chemical composition of its rock creates a
wide range of colors. A short
trail follows the gorge to a
thunderous waterfall, and can
be combined with the trail to
the Paint Pots, iron-rich
mineral springs that bubble
up and stain the water and
earth orange-yellow. The
highway exits the park near
Radium Hot Springs
(Canada's largest) at the base
of dramatic Sinclair Canyon.

Lake Agnes

Park in the Lake Louise parking lot and make your way to the lakeshore promenade for exceptional water level views of the landscape and the Château Lake Louise hotel.

With the water on your left, walk along the lakefront until the footpath splits. Take the right-hand fork climbing immediately from the water's edge.

After 1.2km (0.7 miles) a fine view of the lake appears on the left (from above the waterline the incredible blue tone is even more apparent). It's a perfect place for a photograph, especially if there are kayakers on the water.

The route takes a tight dog-leg here.

The path reaches a plateau after 1.9km (1.1 miles), where you can stop and admire Mirror Lake, backed by a wall of rock and surrounded by shady trees. From here there are two routes to Lake Agnes.

Take the footpath right from the lake, which sweeps around the east.

Enjoy the views east across the broad sweep of Bow Valley to the mountains on its far flank (you'll see the green strips on the mountain sides that in winter are the Lake Louise ski runs).

The path then swings left, west of the Little Beehive rock formation, before the final climb to Lake Agnes, a steep flight of steps to the right of a rock wall often turned into a waterfall with overflow from the lake.

Once you've climbed the steps you will see Lake Agnes's pretty setting, with a curtain of peaks on all sides and the Big Beehive rock formation to your left. Take a break before returning the way you came.

Distance
4km (2.5 miles)

Time
2 hours

Start point
Lake Louise Car Park
✚ 29 B2

End point
Lake Agnes Tea House
✚ 29 B2

Lunch
Lake Agnes Tea House ($–$$)
☎ 403/522-3511

Note:
The path has some steep sections. The upper part follows the same route as the horse trek route to the Tea House, so take care around the horses.

The good, sometimes steep, path is well rewarded by the fine views at the top

🏕 29 B2
ℹ️ Visitor Centre
✉️ Samson Mall, Lake
  Louise, Alberta
☎️ 403/522-3833
🍴 Bill Peyto's Café (➤ 93)
  or the Station Restaurant
  at Lake Louise (➤ 93)

www.skilouise.com/summer
Lake Louise Gondola
✉️ Off Whitehorn Road
☎️ 403/522-3555
🕐 Daily 8–5, Jun to mid-
  Sep; 8.30–4

*Kelowna's marina on
Lake Okanagan*

www.thompsonokanagan.com
🏕 29 B2
ℹ️ Thompson Okanagan
  Tourism Association
✉️ 1332 Water Street,
  Kelowna, BC
☎️ 250/860-5999, 800/567-
  2275 (toll-free)
🍴 De Montreuil, 368 Bernard
  Avenue, Kelowna ($$)

British Columbia Wine Centre
✉️ 888 Westminster Avenue,
  Penticton, BC
☎️ 250/490-2006

Historic O'Keefe Ranch
✉️ Vernon, BC
☎️ 250/542-7868
🕐 Daily May–Oct
💲 Moderate

44

LAKE LOUISE AND MORAINE LAKE

Few sights can compare to Lake Louise, a peerless body of water hidden in the mountains. This sapphire lake, backed by mountains, glaciers and tumbling forests, was named in honor of Queen Victoria's daughter, Princess Louise Caroline Alberta, who was married to the Governor General of Canada. The world-famous Fairmont Château Lake Louise Hotel (➤ 101), begun in 1890, dominates its eastern shore. Vivid turquoise waters surround it at one end, magnificent Victoria Glacier is at the other, and there are soaring mountains all around.

There's a viewing area in front of the hotel that gives a superb view over the lake toward the mountains. You'll get a better view from the **Lake Louise Gondola**, a cable-car that runs up Mount Whitehorn (2,668m/8,753ft). From here you can see over a dozen glaciers.

Fewer people visit Moraine Lake, 13km (8 miles) to the south of Lake Louise on Moraine Lake Road, but it's equally as beautiful as its more famous neighbor. The "Jewel of the Rockies" lies at the foot of the stupendous snow-dusted Wenckchemna Mountains. (This scene used to appear on the Canadian $20 bill.) The best stroll is along the lakeshore; the best walk is to Consolation Lake, 3.2km (2 miles) away.

OKANAGAN VALLEY

This region of low hills, mild-watered lakes and pastoral countryside centers on the towns of Vernon, Kelowna and Penticton, ranged north to south along Okanagan Lake. Its mild, almost Mediterranean climate is perfect for fruit growing, which accounts for the vineyards and orchards. Many of the wineries offer tours and tastings and can be visited by following the Okanagan Wine Route. The **British Columbia Wine Centre** at Penticton has information.

Kelowna is the hub of activity. Its name derives from the First Nations word for grizzly bear, which, in fact, referred to the grizzled appearance of an early settler and not the animal. The town's location midway along the lakeshore gives it access to a full range of watersports, from windsurfing to parasailing. Equipment and boats can be rented from several marinas.

Eleven kilometers (7 miles) to the north of Vernon is the **Historic O'Keefe Ranch**, a collection of original pioneer buildings and a museum that give a taste of ranching life in the 19th century.

Forest-clad mountains sweep down to Cameron Lake in Waterton Lakes National Park

WATERTON LAKES NATIONAL PARK ✪✪

First established in 1895, Waterton Lakes National Park, with its unusual geology, rare wild flowers and abundant wildlife, is today recognized as a biosphere reserve. Rising abruptly out of the prairies, this rare gem protects 521sq km (200sq miles) of the Canadian Rockies in Southwest Alberta, close to the US border. Choose from a wide range of sporting possibilities or over 160km (100 miles) of trails, with opportunities for day and half-day hikes from Waterton townsite. A popular excursion is to walk across the US border (documentation needed) on the Waterton Lakeshore Trail (13km/8 miles) to Goat Haunt in Montana's Glacier National Park. Two specially built scenic roads, the Akamina Parkway (20km/12 miles) and the Red Rock Canyon Parkway (14km/8.5 miles), which leads through a dramatic 20-m (66-ft) deep iron-red gorge, are both accessed from close to Waterton. The highlight of the park's chain of sparkling lakes, carved out of the rock by ancient glaciers, is Upper Waterton Lake; at close to 150m (492ft) it's the deepest in the Canadian Rockies.

www.pc.gc.ca/pn-np/ab/waterton
✚ 29 C1
ℹ Park Administrative Office
✉ 215 Mount View Road, Waterton, Alberta
☎ 403/859-2224

🍴 Cafés and restaurants in Waterton townsite ($–$$$)

WELLS GRAY PROVINCIAL PARK ✪✪✪

Wells Gray is perhaps the finest of all BC's many mountain parks. Access begins at Clearwater where a 60-km (37-mile) road enters and heads north, passing mountain viewpoints, mighty waterfalls, crashing rivers and thick forests. Most sights are accessed from this road.

Eight kilometers (5 miles) from Clearwater, just after the main road crosses the park boundary, a short trail leads via a winding side road to 61-m (200-ft) Spahats Falls, with its brightly colored layers of pink-gray volcanic rock. Green Mountain Lookout has sensational views of the whole park. Dawson Falls is a powerful short but wide cascade, and farther along is Helmcken Falls. At over twice the height of Niagara Falls, they are the park's centerpiece. Here the water cascades into a deep-cut, tree-fringed bowl in a single graceful plume. The park offers great hiking in summer and skiing in winter, but virtually no services, so fill up with gas and take enough picnic supplies.

www.wellsgray.ca
✚ 29 B2
ℹ Clearwater Visitor Infocentre
✉ 425 E Yellowhead Highway (Highway 5), BC
☎ 250/674-2646
🕐 Daily 8–8, Jun–Aug; 9–4, rest of year
🍴 Clearwater ($–$$$)
💷 Visitor Centre free; park inexpensive

45

www.mywhistler.com;
www.tourismwhistler.com

29 A2

Tourism Whistler

4010 Whistler Way, BC

604/938-2769

Several departures daily
from Vancouver and
Vancouver airport

Small charter planes from
Vancouver

WHISTLER

The European-style resort of Whistler lies 120km (75 miles) north of Vancouver amid stunning mountain scenery and is one of North America's finest ski destinations, with abundant snow, a long season, excellent amenities, superlative scenery, high-speed lifts, cable-cars and incredible downhill runs. It is to host the Winter Olympic Games in 2010.

This weekend playground for Vancouverites, nestling between the peaks of Whistler and Blackcomb mountains, is only two and a half hours from the city on the Sea to Sky Highway. It has a range of summer activities too, including golf, mountain biking, fishing, rollerblading and even skiing on Blackcomb's Horstmann Glacier. Garibaldi Provincial Park, just south, draws hikers and mountain bikers.

www.parkscanada.gc.ca/
pn-np/bc/yoho

29 B2

Yoho Visitor Center

Highway 1, 1.5km
(1 mile) east of Field, BC

250/343-6783

Daily 9–7, Jul–Aug; 9–5,
mid-May to Jun and Sep;
reduced hours Oct to
mid-May

Emerald Lake Lodge
($–$$$)

YOHO NATIONAL PARK

This stunning park with its snow-topped mountains, silent forests, spectacular waterfalls and roaring rivers deserves its name – Yoho is a Cree word that means "awesome." On the flanks of the western Rockies, abutting Banff and Kootenay national parks, it is bisected by the scenic TransCanada Highway, which climbs parallel to the railroad from Alberta to the BC boundary at Kicking Horse Pass (1,625m/5,330ft). At the heart of Yoho is Field, the park's only settlement, and two side roads close by give access to some of the park's best trails.

The major draws to the park are the lakes, waterfalls and the Spiral Tunnels. Sparkling Emerald Lake has one of the prettiest vistas anywhere in the park and is perfect for canoeing. Eight kilometers (5 miles) east of Field are the Spiral Tunnels, a pair of figure-eight tunnels that curl around to relieve the steep gradient. People gather to watch the spectacular sight of the front end of incredibly long freight trains emerging from one part of the mountain while the rear has still to enter the tunnel.

On the slopes of Mount Dennis are the famous 530-million-year-old Burgess Shales fossil beds, which have yielded the petrified remains of around 170 species of soft-bodied creatures. Access to this UNESCO World Heritage Site is restricted – contact the visitor center for details.

Information board at the Spiral Tunnels viewpoint, showing the course of the railroad tracks

At 381m (1,250ft), Takakkaw Falls, fed by the meltwaters of the Waputik Icefield, are some of the highest highway-accessible falls in North America, dropping in a series of magnificent cascades.

Icefields Parkway

This magnificent drive between Lake Louise and Jasper takes you through some of the most majestic scenery in the Canadian Rockies (▶ 19).

Take Route 1 north, then the right exit for Route 93 (Icefields Parkway) just north of Lake Louise village (stop at the ticket office for a park pass if you don't already have one).

You'll pass tiny Hector Lake just after the ticket office, but the first important landmark is Crowfoot Glacier, off to the left 34km (21 miles) from Lake Louise.

About 6.4km (4 miles) farther is a left turn to Peyto Lake Viewpoint (▶ 24).

From the parking area it is an easy 20-minute stroll to probably the most breathtaking viewpoint in the Rockies.

After 72km (45 miles) there is parking for Mistaya Canyon. In another 5km (3 miles) you will reach Saskatchewan River Crossing.

Here you can get refreshments, accommodations and the last gas until Jasper.

The parkway follows the North Saskatchewan River, with jagged peaks on either side.

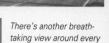

Cirrus Mountain is on the right (parking on the left) before you reach a huge curve in the road. From the parking lot at the top you get a great view down the valley. The 2.5-km (1.5-mile) steep walk along Parker Ridge leads to great views of the Saskatchewan Glacier.

Past Parker Ridge cross from Banff National Park into Jasper National Park. Nearly 10km (6 miles) later you reach the Columbia Icefield Centre, where you can get glacier trips.

At North Columbia Icefield the mountains recede a little as the road follows the wider flood plain of the Sunwapta River. Look out for Sunwapta Falls and Athabasca Falls.

From Athabasca Falls it's 29km (18 miles) to Jasper (▶ 42).

Distance
230km (143 miles)

Time
One day, two if you include longer walks and the Athabasca Glacier trip

Start point
Lake Louise village
✚ 29 B2

End point
Jasper
✚ 29 B2

Lunch
Eat at the Station Restaurant at Lake Louise ($$–$$$) (▶ 93), or stock up with food and drink for a picnic

There's another breath-taking view around every corner

47

The Pacific Coast

The most westerly part of Western Canada lies beside the spectacularly beautiful but wild Pacific Ocean – there's little "pacific" about it here! Deeply indented by fjords and surrounded by towering peaks, the coast is rugged, with a multitude of islands offshore. The largest and best known is Vancouver Island in the south. In the north lies the Queen Charlotte archipelago, mist-shrouded home of the Haida. Between them, the islands supply the protection for the Inside Passage waterway and, penetrating deep inland, the river valleys of the Skeena and the Bella Coola offer dramatic scenery. The Pacific Coast also offers the stately capital of British Columbia, Victoria. Set on a beautiful harbor, with views across the Strait of Juan de Fuca to the mountains of Washington State, USA, it is a charming, fascinating and immensely walkable city.

> *'Real estate agents recommend it as a little piece of England...but no England is set in any such sea or so fully charged with the mystery of the larger ocean beyond.'*
>
> RUDYARD KIPLING (on Victoria)
> *Letters to my Family (1907)*

───────●───────

Opposite: *visitors are dwarfed by the huge hardwood trees of Cathedral Grove*

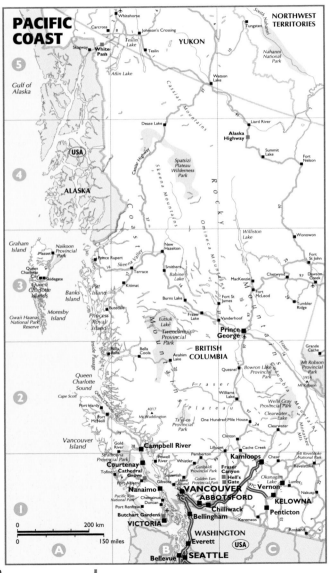

PACIFIC COAST

5

4

3

2

1

A **B** **C**

NORTHWEST TERRITORIES

YUKON

Whitehorse

Carcross

Johnson's Crossing

Tungsten

Skagway

White Pass

Teslin Lake

Teslin

Nahanni National Park

Atlin Lake

Gulf of Alaska

Watson Lake

Cassiar Mountains

Liard River

Alaska Highway

Summit Lake

Fort Nelson

Dease Lake

Cassiar Highway

USA

ALASKA

Spatsizi Plateau Wilderness Park

Skeena Mountains

R O C K Y

Williston Lake

Wonowon

Fort St John

Graham Island

Naikoon Provincial Park

Masset

Queen Charlotte

Sidegate

Queen Charlotte Islands

Prince Rupert

Skeena Valley

New Hazelton

Smithers

Babine Lake

Omineca Mountains

MacKenzie

Fort McLeod

Chetwynd

Dawson Creek

Banks Island

Pitt Island

Terrace

Kitimat

Burns Lake

Fort St James

Tumbler Ridge

Gwaii Haanas National Park Reserve

Moresby Island

Butedale

Princess Royal Island

Eutsuk Lake

Tweedsmuir Provincial Park

Fraser Lake

Vanderhoof

Prince George

Grande Cache

Inside Passage

Bella Bella

Bella Coola

Anahim Lake

BRITISH COLUMBIA

Fraser

Quesnel

Bowron Lake Provincial Park

Mt Robson Provincial Park

3954 Mt Robson

Queen Charlotte Sound

Cape Scott

Williams Lake

Wells Gray Provincial Park

Clearwater Lake

Monashee Mts

Port Hardy

Port McNeill

4017 Mt Waddington

P l a t e a u

One Hundred Mile House

Clearwater

Vancouver Island

Gold River

Strathcona Provincial Park

Ts'yl-os Provincial Park

Clinton

Lillooet

Cache Creek

Kamloops

Chase

Mt Revelstoke National Park

Revelstoke

Campbell River

Courtenay

Cathedral Grove

Powell River

Pemberton

Whistler

Squamish

Howe Sound

Garibaldi Provincial Park

Fraser Canyon

Hell's Gate

Okanagan Lake

Lumby

Vernon

Nakusp

Tofino

Port Alberni

Gibsons

Golden Ears Provincial Park

KELOWNA

Pacific Rim National Park

Nanaimo

Chemainus

Duncan

VANCOUVER

ABBOTSFORD

Chilliwack

Penticton

Port Renfrew

Butchart Gardens

Bellingham

Keremeos

Rossland

VICTORIA

WASHINGTON

Everett

Bellevue

SEATTLE

USA

0 — 200 km

0 — 150 miles

50

Victoria

Victoria, capital of British Columbia, sits on the southernmost tip of Vancouver Island, with one of the finest natural harbors in the world. This former Hudson's Bay Company trading post (1843) prospered in the 1860s as prospectors stopped off en route to the Chilcotin gold fields. It was named in honor of Queen Victoria, and the city has maintained its strong links with Britain.

Today this small, sedate city with its quaint English air, leafy old town, delightful old-fashioned shopping streets and exquisite harbor is a world away from the hustle and bustle of most provincial capitals. It's an easy place to explore on foot – most of what you will want to see is concentrated on or around the Inner Harbour and the Old Town. Foremost among Victoria's attractions are the Royal British Columbia Museum (▶ 53), one of Canada's finest, and the fascinating Maritime Museum (▶ 52).

Craigdarroch Castle, on the outskirts at Rockland, is the Victorian Gothic home of coal magnate Robert Dunsmuir, who moved to Canada from Scotland in 1851. It has some of the finest stained and leaded glass in western Canada and many flamboyant architectural features.

Whale-watching trips from the harbor are among the most popular activites, with opportunities for spotting orcas (killer whales), grays and humpbacks, harbor and Dall's porpoises, harbor and elephant seals, and sea lions.

www.tourismvictoria.com
- 50 B1
- Victoria Visitor Information Centre
- 812 Wharf Street
- 250/953-2033
- Daily 8.30–8, May–Sep; 9–5, rest of year

www.craigdarrochcastle.com
Craigdarroch Castle
- 1050 Joan Crescent
- 250/592-5323
- Daily
- Moderate

The Fairmont Empress Hotel, overlooking the harbor, is a Victoria icon

What to See in Victoria

DOWNTOWN VICTORIA ✪✪

North of the Inner Harbour (▶ below) is the downtown area, a delightful mix of historic buildings, stores, restaurants and mock-English pubs. It has a "village" atmosphere and is very walkable. The Sticky Wicket is by far the best of Victoria's pubs, and has become a bit of an institution.

Victoria's Chinatown, the third largest in Canada, centers on Fisgard Street and tiny Fan Tan Alley, named after a Chinese card game and reputedly the world's narrowest street. Once a hotbed of brothels, bars and opium dens, it is no longer a place to avoid and is full of quaint Chinese stores, galleries and New-Age boutiques. The two stone chimeras (mythical beasts) by the Gate of Harmonious Interest were a gift from Suzhou in China. It is said they will come to life when an honest politican walks between them.

There's little to the north worth exploring, so head south on Government Street or Wharf Street (▶ 54, walk) toward the Inner Harbour.

INNER HARBOUR ✪✪

The lovely Inner Harbour is the atmospheric heart of Victoria, a sweeping waterfront fringing the city's downtown (▶ above). A stroll around its promenade is a great way to take in several of the city's best-known attractions. It's particularly pleasant in the evening when filled with a lively mix of people and street entertainers. It's also fun to take a ride on one of the tiny ferries that buzz around the harbor. Opposite the Infocentre on Wharf Street is the Fairmont Empress Hotel, designed by Francis Rattenbury, which opened in 1908 and has been a city landmark ever since. The elegant afternoon tea is deservedly popular. Other attractions on the harbor include sightseeing cruises and whale-watching trips.

MARITIME MUSEUM ✪✪

The Maritime Museum, a cut above most museums of its kind, is home to an exquisite collection of artifacts that explore British Columbia's seafaring history. Housed in the historic 1889 Provincial Law Courts on Bastion Square, its six galleries – Exploration, Commerce, Adventure, Passenger, Government Fleets and BC Ferries – contain fascinating maritime memorabilia such as model ships, uniforms, old photographs and ships' bells. Two rare globes that were created after Captain Cook returned to England with new mapping information are among the prize possessions. The galleries themselves are superbly decorated with beautiful woodwork, including walnut, cedar and oak, and this makes a particularly attractive setting for the exhibitions.

🍴 Cafés in Bastion Square ($–$$); Sticky Wicket (▶ 97)

Ancient and modern art fronts the Royal BC Museum

🍴 Tea at the Fairmont Empress Hotel (▶ 102)

---

www.mmbc.bc.ca
 28 Bastion Square
☎ 250/385-4222
🕐 Daily 9.30–5 mid-Sep to mid-Jun; 9.30–4.30 rest of year
 Good
👋 Moderate

PARLIAMENT BUILDINGS

The beautiful, domed 1893 Parliament Buildings, the seat of BC's Legislative Assembly, overlook the Inner Harbour and are worthy of a visit for their modern Gothic Revival-style architecture (by prolific architect Francis Rattenbury), a stately reminder of British colonial influence. You can take a free guided tour inside, and when the Legislature is in session you can sit in the public gallery and watch, but the main attraction is the ornate exterior detail. Various dignitaries from the province's past adorn the façade. A gilded statue of George Vancouver, the first European to sail around Vancouver Island, tops the central dome, while a statue of Queen Victoria overlooks the formal gardens at the front. At night the entire building is illuminated by thousands of tiny lights.

www.legis.gov.bc.ca
✉ 501 Belleville Street
☎ 250/387-3046
🕐 Daily 8.30–4.30, summer; Mon–Fri 8.30–4.30 rest of year
♿ Good
🎟 Free

Above: *Twinkling lights illuminate and outline the Parliament Buildings at night*

ROYAL BRITISH COLUMBIA MUSEUM

The superlative RBCM is regarded as one of the top ten museums in North America and really deserves two days to do it justice. Its three galleries showcase the natural history of the region, provincial history and the Pacific Northwest's First Nations with excellent displays and some dramatic dioramas.

The Natural History Gallery is divided into two separate sections: Living Land, Living Sea opens in dramatic style with a life-size woolly mammoth, while the state-of-the-art Open Ocean, with its dark tunnels, takes you on a gripping submarine tour of the sea and deep ocean. Think twice if you are claustrophobic.

The Modern History Gallery explores British Columbia's history after the arrival of European settlers. It's most impressive exhibit is the re-creation of a turn-of-the-20th-century street, complete with cobblestones and rumbling train sounds.

The centerpiece of the First Nations Gallery is the reconstructed, full-size ceremonial longhouse of Chief Kwakwabalasami, with an excellent audiovisual display. Every August the museum holds a three-day outdoor festival celebrating BC's First Nations.

www.rbcm.gov.bc.ca
✉ 675 Belleville Street
☎ 250/356-7226, 888/447-7877 (toll-free in North America)
🕐 Museum: daily 9–5; IMAX: daily 9–9
🍴 Café ($)
♿ Excellent
🎟 Moderate

Downtown Victoria

Distance
2.4km (1.5 miles)

Time
1.5 hours. Allow extra time for window-shopping, refreshment stops and visiting museums

Start/end point
Inner Harbour Infocentre
⊞ 50 B1

Lunch
Pagliacci's (▶ 97)

The entrance to the Market Square in the Old Town

This walk takes you through the heart of old Victoria, touching on the harbor area, Market Square and Chinatown.

From the Infocentre head north on Government Street, ducking into the smaller streets that run across it from east to west. The first is Courtney Street, followed by Broughton then Fort.

At 822 Fort Street is the unusual Flag Shop, which makes and sells a huge variety of flags, pendants and crests. On Broughton Street, you can drop into The Wine Barrel, at No. 644 on the corner of Broad Street, for top British Columbia and other wines.

Turn left up Broad Street, then left on Fort Street to bring you back to Government Street.

Note No. 1022 on the west side of the street at the corner of Fort Street, formerly the heart of Fort Victoria, built in 1843 by the Hudson's Bay Company.

Continue north along Government Street, past View Street on your right.

The next right is Trounce Alley, a tempting retreat filled with old gaslights and colorful hanging baskets, with a medley of specialty stores and boutiques.

Turn left at Broad Street, cross Yates Street and then turn left at the top of Broad Street on Johnson Street. Cross Government Street and a short way down the westerly continuation of Johnson Street on the right is an entrance to the stores, restaurants and bars of Market Square.

Explore Market Square, then return to Johnson Street and turn right. Turn right on Store Street and then right on Fisgard Street, focus of Victoria's Chinatown. Halfway down Fisgard Street on the right is Fan Tan Alley (▶ 52).

Return to Store Street and turn left. At Johnson Street turn right, then left when you reach Wharf Street. After about 175m (574ft) detour left around Bastion Square then continue on Wharf Street, to return to the Inner Harbour.

Light filters through the dense Pacific rain forest at Cathedral Grove

What to See on the Pacific Coast

BUTCHART GARDENS (➤ 17, TOP TEN)

CATHEDRAL GROVE ✪✪
Although this 136-ha (336-acre) park is officially called MacMillan Provincial Park, most people know it as Cathedral Grove, and it's famous for its giant 800-year-old Douglas fir trees, the largest of which has a circumference of 9m (29ft) and stands 76m (249ft) high. Well-marked trails lead through these majestic stands of forest, and following the south loop you really do feel as if you are within a mighty cathedral, formed by the high canopy of elegant, moss-draped trees. North of the highway a trail leads to Cameron Lake, where you can swim or have a picnic, or hike in neighboring Little Qualicum Falls Park, west of Parksville, with impressive waterfalls that cascade down into a rocky gorge in a beautiful forest setting.

www.britishcolumbia. com/parksandtrails
✚ 50 B1
⊠ Off Highway 4, 29km (18 miles) west of Parksville
🕐 Daily dawn–dusk
♿ Main routes of interpretive trail: good
🎫 Free

CHEMAINUS ✪✪✪
The small, former logging town of Chemainus, 80km (50 miles) north of Victoria, is Canada's largest outdoor art gallery. Over 250,000 visitors come each year to view the fascinating collection of murals that adorn the walls and buildings downtown. The first were commissioned in 1983 to revitalize the town after it began to decline following the closure of its sawmill. There are now 34 murals, with subjects ranging from a 19th-century brigantine to portraits of First Nations people. The murals are scattered around the town and as you move from one to the next you will learn all about Chemainus's history. In July and August the town celebrates its annual Festival of Murals.

The town itself is a delight, with its pretty painted clapboard houses, antiques shops, boutiques and coffee houses. It is also the departure point for ferry rides to two little islands nearby, Thetis and Kuper.

www.chemainus.com
✚ 50 B1
ℹ Visitor InfoCentre
⊠ 9796 Willow Street
☎ 250/246-3944

Chemainus is known as the "Town of Murals"

HOWE SOUND (➤ 18, TOP TEN)

www.tourismnanaimo.com
🏠 50 B1
ℹ️ 3Tourism Nanaimo
✉️ 2290 Bowen Road
☎️ 250/756-0106

www.nanaimomuseum.ca
Nanaimo District Museum
✉️ 100 Cameron Street
☎️ 250/753-1821
🕐 Daily 9–5, May–Sep;
Tue–Sat 9–5, rest of year
💵 Inexpensive

www.pacificrimtourism.ca
🏠 50 B1
ℹ️ 3Pacific Rim Tourism
✉️ 3100 Kingsway, The
Station, Port Alberni
☎️ 250/723-7529

ℹ️ Pacific Rim National Park
Office
✉️ 2185 Ocean Terrace
Road, Ucluelet, BC
☎️ 250/726-7721

🍴 Cafés and restaurants at
Ucluelet and Tofino
($–$$$)

Above: *driftwood littering
Long Beach is testament
to the winter storms that
batter this coast*

NANAIMO ✪✪

Nanaimo is Vancouver Island's second biggest city, and the attractive waterfront is always busy with freighters, barges and fishing boats. Follow the Harbourside Walkway and call in at the **Bastion**, an original Hudson's Bay Company fort and now part of the nearby **Nanaimo District Museum**, which celebrates the town's major industry – coal. It also gives an insight into early coastal life on the island and has reproduction castings from Petroglyph Provincial Park. During the last weekend in July, the town hosts the annual Great International World Bathtub Race over the 53km (33 miles) across Georgia Strait to Kitsilano Beach.

PACIFIC RIM NATIONAL PARK ✪✪✪

This outstanding park, a combination of mountains, rain forest and wild coastal scenery, is one of the main reasons visitors come to Vancouver Island. It stretches for 128km (80 miles) along the western coast and incorporates the wild and beautiful Broken Islands in Barkley Sound, reached by charter boat (daily Apr–Sep) from Port Alberni. Back on the mainland, Long Beach is a glorious 16-km (10-mile) strand of windblown beaches and crashing waves. Tofino and Ucluelet are the main towns at its northern and southern ends respectively. The popular but challenging 77-km (48-mile) West Coast Trail, originally an escape route for shipwrecked sailors to the interior, is not for novices.

DID YOU KNOW?

Just south of Nanaimo is tiny 2-ha (5-acre) Petroglyph Provincial Park, where exquisite symbolic etchings of mythical sea creatures, animals and human figures were carved into the rock as long as 10,000 years ago.

PRINCE RUPERT AND THE SKEENA VALLEY ✪✪

Prince Rupert first developed as a Hudson's Bay Company post at the mouth of the Skeena River. Today it is the last ferry stop before Alaska on the Inside Passage (➤ 58) from Port Hardy on Vancouver Island, surrounded by vast mountains, deep-cut fjords and a sprinkling of tiny islands. The original 1905 buildings along the waterfront at Cow Bay have been renovated into stores, galleries and restaurants. Leave time to visit the fascinating **Museum of Northern British Columbia**, which has an excellent collection of First Nations art and features a traditional longhouse. In summer it runs 2-hour archeology trips to the harbor (phone for details).

The Skeena Valley – "river of mists," or 'Ksan in the Tsimshian language – can be visited as part of the Inside Passage tour (➤ 58), by car, VIA Rail or bus from Prince George. Take a detour to New Hazelton to see **'Ksan**, a traditional Gitxsan village, which was created to preserve this rapidly vanishing culture. The site features several tribal longhouses and what is reputedly the world's largest standing totem pole; you will see other fine examples along the way.

QUEEN CHARLOTTE ISLANDS (HAIDA GWAII) ✪✪

These islands lie 128km (80 miles) west of Prince Rupert across the Hecate Strait. Called Haida Gwaii ("islands of the people") by the Haida people, they offer some of the most remote coastal landscape in Canada – snow-topped mountains and sheer-sided fjords, mist-shrouded forests and windswept sandy beaches. This fascinating archipelago comprises the two larger islands of Graham and Moresby and 150 smaller ones.

Graham Island, the largest and most northerly island, is also the most accessible, with a ferry from Prince Rupert to Skidegate. Here the **Haida Gwaii Museum** showcases the traditional Haida culture and history, and the geology of the islands. To the west, Queen Charlotte City is the administrative center for the islands.

Sandspit is the only settlement on Moresby Island and starting point for the Gwaii Haanas National Park, which covers most of the island, preserving its dense rain forest. Access is only by boat and floatplane, reservations are required and you must attend an orientation session. The easiest way is to take a local chartered trip.

---

www.tourismprincerupert.com
- 50 A3
- Visitor Centre
- Suite 100, 215 Cow Bay Road
- ☎ 250/624-5637
- From Port Hardy, Vancouver Island

www.museumofnorthernbc.com
Museum of Northern BC
- ✉ 100 1st Avenue West
- ☎ 250/624-3207
- ⏰ Mon–Sat 9–8, Sun 9–5, Jun–Aug; Mon–Sat 9–5, rest of year
- ✋ Moderate

'Ksan
- ✉ New Hazelton, BC
- ☎ 250/842-5544
- ⏰ Daily; tours summer only
- ✋ Inexpensive; tours expensive

Primitive artwork adorns a building at 'Ksan

---

www.qcislands.net/tourism
- 50 A3
- Queen Charlotte Visitor Centre
- ✉ 3220 Wharf Street, Queen Charlotte City, BC
- ☎ 250/559-8316
- BC Ferries from Prince Rupert to Skidegate
- ✈ Daily flights from Vancouver and Prince Rupert to Sandspit

Haida Gwaii Museum
- ✉ Qay'llnagaay, Skidegate
- ☎ 250/559-4643
- ⏰ Mon–Fri 10–5, Sat–Sun 1–5. Closed Sun Sep–May, also Tue Dec–May
- ✋ Inexpensive

The Inside Passage

Distance 288km (179 miles)

Time 15 hours

Start point
Port Hardy, Vancouver Island
✚ 50 B2

End point
Prince Rupert
✚ 50 B3

Refreshments
Aboard ship

Orcas (killer whales) are permanent residents on the BC coastline, joined every year by migrating whales of other species

The Inside Passage is one of the world's most dramatic voyages, offering the chance to see migrating whales and other marine life.

An hour after leaving Port Hardy the boat sails port (left) of tiny Pine Island, where a lighthouse marks the main entrance to the Inside Passage.

Beyond here is the most exposed section of the journey. The lighthouse on Egg Island has suffered severe damage several times since it was established in 1898. Up ahead the channel narrows and the boat enters FitzHugh Sound.

At its northern end the ship takes a port turn between Hunter and Denny islands, then cruises starboard (right) of Campbell Island, passing McLoughlin Bay, also known as Bella Bella.

Dryad Point marks the northern tip of Campbell Island and the ship feels the full force of the ocean passing through exposed Milbanke Sound before turning to starboard toward Boat Bluff, the halfway point. The next four hours offer the most spectacular experience of the journey as the ship plies the narrowest section – a long sheer-sided fjord stretching off into the distance.

Ten hours from Port Hardy, Butedale comes into view on the port side.

Founded in 1919, Butedale was one of the longest-lived fish cannery villages along the coast, only ceasing production in 1956. Hartley Bay, a traditional Tsimshian First Nations village, marks the southern tip of Grenville Channel, a 64-km (40-mile) long section whose narrowest point is just 500m (1,640ft) wide. Hartley Bay is only accessible by boat or floatplane and is a favorite anchorage for recreational sailors during the summer.

At the northern mouth of the Grenville Channel, on the port side, is Oona River. From here it's only another two hours to Prince Rupert (► 57), passing the bulk shipping terminal on Ridley Island on the starboard side shortly before docking.

The Prairies

Canada's Prairie provinces – Manitoba, Saskatchewan and Alberta from east to west – are not just the flat grasslands that famously stretch to the horizon. They actually rise in stages, from sea level around Hudson's Bay, through the Manitoba Escarpment and the Missouri Coteau, to a height of more than 1,200m (3,937ft) near the foothills of the Rocky Mountains. The region incorporates a variety of landscapes – the frozen wastes of the northern tundra, the canyons and dramatic moonscapes of the Alberta Badlands, the uplands of the Cypress Hills and, of course, those huge wheatfields and cattle ranges.

You get an overall view of the enormity of the Prairies from a plane, but take the VIA Rail train from Toronto to Edmonton or drive the Yellowhead Highway or TransCanada for a more hands-on experience. Vast Prairie skies, stunning sunsets and the shimmering colors of the Northern Lights are a major complement to this wide, open land – a region that drew a diverse cultural mix of immigrants from across Europe.

'The Lord said 'Let there be Wheat' and Saskatchewan was born.'

STEPHEN LEACOCK
My Discovery of America (1937)

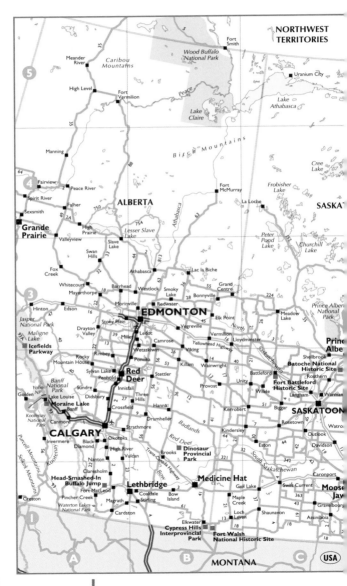

THE PRAIRIES

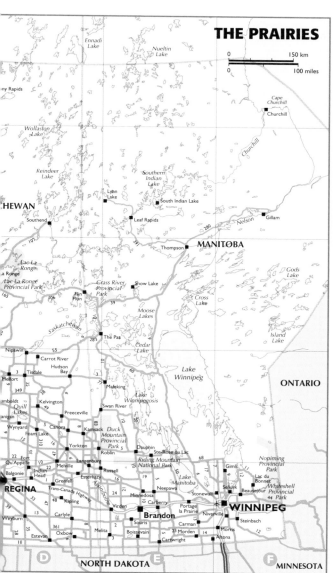

0 | 150 km
0 | 100 miles

ny Rapids

Ennadi Lake

Nueltin Lake

Wollaston Lake

Cape Churchill
Churchill

Reindeer Lake

Southern Indian Lake

Lynn Lake

South Indian Lake

Churchill

Churchill

.HEWAN

Southend

Leaf Rapids

Nelson

Gillam

107

391

Thompson

MANITOBA

280

Lac La Ronge
a Ronge

Lac La Ronge Provincial Park

165

106

Grass River Provincial Park

Snow Lake

Cross Lake

Gods Lake

Flin Flon

39

Moose Lakes

Saskatchewan

81

The Pas

Cedar Lake

Island Lake

Nipawin

55

Carrot River

Lake Winnipeg

ONTARIO

Melfort

Tisdale

Hudson Bay

3

Mafeking

60

283

349

33

Kelvington

49

Preeceville

Lake Winnipegosis

imboldt
Quill Lakes

5

Swan River

Wynyard

Foam Lake

Canora

8

Kamsack

Duck Mountain Provincial Park

Dauphin

Ste-Rose du Lac

68

Nopiming Provincial Park

Gimli

anigan

9

310

Yorkton

Roblin

5

Riding Mountain National Park

Lake Manitoba

12

22
Fort Qu'Appelle

10

Melville

Langenburg

Russell

19

Neepawa

Stonewall

Selkirk

Lac du Bonne

Beausejour

Whiteshell Provincial Park

Balgonie

Indian Head

1

Grenfell

Esterhazy

16

24

Minnedosa

Carberry

Portage la Prairie

Niverville

WINNIPEG

REGINA

Trans-Canada Highway

33

48

Kipling

Virden

2

Souris

Brandon

Morden

14

Morris

Steinbach

29

Weyburn

13

Carlyle

8

361

Melita

Boissevain

3

29

Cartwright

Altona

12

28

35

Estevan

Oxbow

18

D
E
F
MINNESOTA

Winnipeg

Capital of Manitoba and "Gateway to the Prairies," Winnipeg began life as a Hudson's Bay Company franchise, though the region was originally inhabited long ago by the Assiniboine and Cree people. It grew with the arrival of the Canadian Pacific Railway in 1881, and from 1901 to 1911 its population increased with an influx of immigrants from Europe, creating today's thriving cosmopolitan city. Winnipeg has beautiful parks, excellent hotels and restaurants, and an underground shopping mall.

Most of its sightseeing attractions are clustered in Downtown, the Forks (to the east), the Centennial Centre and Ukranian Cultural Centre (to the north), and St. Boniface (across the river to the east). In the churchyard of St. Boniface Basilica is the grave of Louis Riel (1844–1885), leader of the Métis – a mixed-race, French-speaking nation – and a famous participant in the Northwest Rebellion. The city's French heritage is best explored in the St. Boniface Museum, Winnipeg's oldest building (494 avenue Tache), with its fascinating collection of Métis-related artifacts.

What to See in Winnipeg

CENTENNIAL CENTRE ✪✪✪

This magnificent complex was built as part of Canada's centennial celebrations in 1967 and is home to the outstanding **Manitoba Museum of Man and Nature** (▶ 21). It also houses Oseredok, the Ukrainian cultural and educational center, with a museum and art gallery devoted to Ukrainian culture, lifestyle, folk art and crafts.

The focus of its lively performing arts center is the Centennial Concert Hall, home of Winnipeg's Royal Ballet (the oldest dance company in Canada), its Opera company and the Winnipeg Symphony Orchestra, in addition to hosting traveling international classical and modern performances.

---

www.tourism.winnipeg.mb.ca
🔲 61 F1
ℹ️ Tourism Winnipeg
✉️ 259 Portage Avenue, Winnipeg, Manitoba
☎ 204/943-1970, 800/665-0204 (toll-free in North America)

Centennial Concert Hall
✉️ 555 Main Street
☎ 204/956-1360, 204/957-0835 (box office)
🕐 Depends on performance
♿ Good
🎫 Depends on performance

www.oseredok.org
Oseredok
✉️ 184 Alexander Avenue E
☎ 204/942-0218
🕐 Mon–Sat 10–4

Monument to Louis Riel, revolutionary leader of the Métis community

62

DOWNTOWN ✪✪

Downtown Winnipeg stretches north and west of the junction of the Red and Assiniboine rivers, and includes the intersection of Portage Avenue and Main Road (reputedly the windiest corner in Canada). Winnipeg Square is the heart of the shopping district, with the Winnipeg Art Gallery (➤ 65) and Winnipeg Commodity Exchange (the only agricultural exchange in Canada) nearby. Also here is the **Dalnavert National Historic District** and the neoclassical Legislative Building, one of the finest public buildings in Canada. The Golden Boy statue on top of the 74-m (243-ft) high dome of the "Ledge" is one of the best-known symbols of Manitoba. It stands 4.1m (13ft) high, weighs 5 tonnes and is covered in 23.5 carat gold. Downtown has many fine urban parks, notably those that line the rivers.

THE EXCHANGE DISTRICT AND MARKET SQUARE ✪✪

The regenerated Exchange District, a National Historic Site, is a lively area of bars, restaurants and nightlife in the city's 19th-century heart. Once a run-down area of warehouses and marshaling yards, it has a wealth of fine early 20th-century architecture. This includes the 1912 Confederation Life building, an early skyscraper; the lavish 1913 Pantages Theatre; the 1903 British Bank of North America; and the 1903 Criterion Hotel, with its rare terra cotta façade.

Between June and September walking tours of the Exchange District and Market Square, lasting between one and two hours, depart from the information center on Old Market Square, a place that becomes a focus for outdoor performances of every kind during the summer.

www.tourism.winnipeg.mb.ca
🛈 279 Portage Avenue
☎ 204/943-1970

Dalnavert National Historic District
✉ 61 Carlton Street
☎ 204/943-2835
🕐 Due to reopen late 2004 – call for information
💲 Inexpensive

www.exchangedistrict.org
🛈 Information Office
✉ 314–63 Albert Street
☎ 204/942-6716

Winnipeg's Exchange District is full of restored old warehouses

Sculpture representing the ancient meeting place that is now The Forks

---

www.theforks.com

📧 1 Forks Market Road

☎ 204/942-6302; 204/957-7618 (events hotline)

🍴 Choice of restaurants and cafés ($–$$$)

♿ Good

🖐 Free

THE FORKS NATIONAL HISTORIC SITE ✪✪✪

Located in the center of Winnipeg, where the Red and Assiniboine rivers meet, is the Forks, originally a meeting place for the First Nations. Today this revitalized district is a gathering place for locals and visitors alike, who come to enjoy its historic landmarks, leafy parks, river walkways and excellent marketplace. Here, former Canadian Pacific Railway buildings have been transformed into a shopping, eating and entertainment complex with interpretive displays, sculptures and a wide range of events for all the family. The riverside walk is a great way to spend a summer's evening, and the waterfront gardens have lots of open-air events.

---

www.
pc.gc.ca/lhn-nhs/mb/fortgarry

📧 5981 Highway 9, Selkirk

☎ 877/534-3678

🕐 Daily 9–5, mid-May to early Sep

🍴 Restaurant ($–$$)

♿ Good

🖐 Moderate

LOWER FORT GARRY ✪✪

The excellent Lower Fort Garry National Historic Park, 32km (20 miles) north of Winnipeg on Highway 9, contains North America's oldest intact stone fur-trading post, founded in 1881. Guides in period costume help visitors to experience life in the mid-1800s. You can talk to the "governor" and his wife up at the Big House, the heart of the complex, and listen to the staff describing their lives as they go about their daily tasks. The visitor reception center shows a movie that gives a good introduction to the history of the fort, which was a key component in the Hudson's Bay Company network. There is also a small but exquisite collection of period artifacts, from First Nations household articles to imported porcelain. Other buildings include warehouses, a granary, a brewery, a sawmill and a well-stocked fur loft.

---

www.childrensmuseum.com

📧 45 Forks Market Road

☎ 204/924-4000

🕐 Daily 9.30–4.30 (also 4.30–8, Fri–Sat)

🍴 Café ($–$$)

♿ Good

🖐 Inexpensive

MANITOBA CHILDREN'S MUSEUM ✪✪

Located at the Forks Historical Site, next to the Johnson Terminal, this terrific museum is an exciting hands-on learning center for children, devoted to fun and make-believe. In the Wonderworks Gallery they can design a city, play with water and make electrical connections. In the Prehistoric Playground they can interact with baby dinosaurs and make a juvenile *T-Rex* come to life. There's a TV studio where they can create and present their own shows, or operate the cameras. It's a family-oriented attraction and the eclectic mixture of historical, scientific and natural displays appeals to children and adults alike.

MANITOBA MUSEUM OF MAN AND NATURE
(▶ 21, TOP TEN)

MENNONITE HERITAGE VILLAGE ✪✪

Around 65,000 Mennonites, members of a Protestant German-speaking sect, live in Manitoba. This authentic re-creation of a typical Mennonite village occupies a 16-ha (37-acre) site near Steinbach, 61km (39.5 miles) southeast of Winnipeg, and is a fascinating introduction to their culture and lifestyle from the 17th century to the present day. Among more than 30 traditional buildings are a windmill, a house-barn, a church, a schoolhouse and a semlin – a crude type of sod and wood house, built as a temporary shelter when the settlers first arrived. There's also a traditional outdoor clay oven where hearty breads and buns are baked. You can sample typical Mennonite fare in the Livery Barn Restaurant, and the general store sells Mennonite crafts, seeds, books and souvenirs.

www.
mennoniteheritagevillage.com
✉ Just north of Steinbach, on Highway 12, Manitoba
☎ 204/326-9661
🕐 Mon–Sat 10–7, Sun noon–6, Jul–Aug; Mon–Sat 10–5, Sun noon–5, May–Jun and Sep. Closed Oct–Apr
🍴 Livery Barn Restaurant ($–$$)
♿ Good
💲 Moderate

Children get a taste of technology-free education at the Mennonite Village

WINNIPEG ART GALLERY ✪✪✪

Winnipeg Art Gallery is one of the city's architectural showpieces and Canada's oldest public gallery. Designed by local architect Gustavo da Roza and built in local Tyndall stone, it resembles a ship rising out of the water. It comprises over 22,500 works, and contains one of the world's largest collections of contemporary Inuit art, with more than 10,000 carvings, prints, drawings and textiles. The gallery also features changing exhibitions by Manitoban, Canadian and international artists, past and present. A highlight is the Gort Collection of Gothic and Northern Renaissance altar paintings and tapestries from the 16th century. An added bonus is the wonderful rooftop café where you can listen to live jazz in the summer while enjoying panoramic views over the city.

www.wag.mb.ca
✉ 300 Memorial Boulevard
☎ 204/786-6641
🕐 Tue–Sun 11–5 (also 5–9 Wed). Closed Mon
🍴 Brio Restaurant ($$)
♿ Good
💲 Moderate

65

Downtown Winnipeg

Distance
7km (4.3 miles)

Time
4 hours (excluding exploring
the attractions)

Start/end point
The Forks
⊞ 61 F1

Lunch
The Forks, Exchange District,
Manitoba Museum, or
Portage Place Shopping
Centre ($–$$$)

This route connects many of Winnipeg's most frequently
visited attractions.

*Start at The Forks (▶ 64). Walk along the
riverside toward the Provencher Bridge and
cross the Red River. Turn right on Tache
Avenue and walk one block to the heart of
Winnipeg's French Quarter.*

Stroll among the ruins of the 1908 St. Boniface Cathedral
and its graveyard, containing the tomb of Louis Riel (▶ 62).

*Recross the river and take the first right, Pioneer
Boulevard. You'll pass the CanWest Global
Park baseball field on your left and walk
underneath the railroad bridge before entering
the Exchange District (▶ 63).*

Explore the network of cobblestone streets. Lombard,
McDermot or Bannatyne avenues will bring you out on to
Main Street to continue your journey.

*Turn right on Main Street. The block after
Market Street leads to the Centennial Concert
Hall (▶ 62) and the Manitoba Museum of
Man and Nature (▶ 21). Cross Main Street
and walk back the way you just came until you
reach the junction with Portage Avenue. Turn
right at Portage, the city's main shopping street.
Continue past Portage Place Shopping Centre
(six blocks along on the right) until you reach
The Bay department store on the left. Turn left
here along Memorial Boulevard.*

On the opposite side of the road to The Bay is the
Winnipeg Art Gallery (▶ 65).

*Continue along Memorial Boulevard and
through the ornamental gardens. After three
blocks cross Broadway to reach the Legislature
Building. Return to Broadway and head right.*

You will see Winnipeg train station at the end of the street.
One block before it is Hotel Fort Garry, on the right, famed
for it's ornate bar and gargantuan Sunday brunch. When
you reach the station on Main Street look to it's right and
you'll see an underpass that leads back to The Forks.

Calgary

From its beginnings as a North West Mounted Police fort in 1875, Calgary has prospered, first on the back of agriculture, and since the 1970s from the area's burgeoning oil and gas industry. This wealth has helped pay for the city's shiny high-rise center, with its mirror skyscrapers, glamorous corporate buildings and urban expressways.

Set in the rolling foothills of the Alberta Rockies, Calgary enjoys a backdrop of gorgeous scenery and is perfectly placed for exploring the mountains to the west, but the city itself deserves a visit too. The terrific Glenbow Museum alone would make it worthwhile, but there is also one of the biggest zoos in Canada, a lively heritage park and a leafy urban park set on an island in the middle of the Bow River.

The Calgary Stampede (► 72) is the city's best-known attraction, ten days of parades and rodeos that draw over a million visitors a year from around the world.

www.tourismcalgary.com
➕ 60 A2
ℹ️ Tourism Calgary
200, 238-11 Avenue SE
☎ 403/263-8510, 800/661-1678 (toll-free in North America)

Calgary's distinctive cityscape features the Calgary Tower and the Saddledome stadium

What to See in Calgary

CALGARY TOWER ✪✪

The 1968 Calgary Tower, in the heart of downtown, is one of the city's most distinctive landmarks. At 193m (633ft) it was once the city's tallest structure, though these days it has been superceded by three others. High-speed elevators take visitors to the top for a great all-round view of the city and its setting. On a clear day you can see as far as the peaks of the Rockies to the west and the rippling prairies stretching away to the east. During the Winter Olympics of 1988, the Olympic torch burned non-stop at the top. The tower lies across the street from the Glenbow Museum (► 69), close to the main shopping malls.

www.calgarytower.com
✉️ 101 9th Avenue SW
☎ 403/266-7171
🕐 Daily 8am–11pm
🍴 Snack bar and revolving restaurant ($–$$$)
♿ Observation deck and restaurant: good
💲 Moderate

67

www.calgaryzoo.org
⊠ 1300 Zoo Road NE
☎ 403/232-9300
🕐 Daily 9–5
🍴 Cafés and kiosks ($)
☎ Good
♿ Moderate

*Above: the giraffe house
at Calgary Zoo has a
décor of murals that
resemble the great
outdoors*

CALGARY ZOO ✪✪

Calgary Zoo covers 32ha (79 acres) to the east of the city and is one of the best zoological gardens in Canada. It has made a strenuous effort to accommodate the animals in as near "natural" habitats as possible, including rain forest, savanna and mountain environments, encompassing Africa, Eurasia and Australian sections. There are also underwater viewing areas for watching fish and marine mammals. Live animals, from gorillas to grizzlies, provide an intriguing and educational experience.

The Prehistoric Park is particularly popular with children, with its displays of life-size dinosaur replicas, model volcano and more than 100 species of plants. Here you can discover what life in western Canada might have been like when these mighty creatures reigned supreme in the swamplands of Alberta. The beautiful Botanical Gardens contain over 4,000 plant species and include a tropical rain forest, an arid garden and butterfly gardens.

www.fortcalgary.ab.ca
⊠ 750 9th Avenue SE
☎ 403/290-1875
🕐 Daily 9–5
🍴 Deane House Restaurant
($–$$); Mess Kitchen
($–$$)
♿ Good
♿ Moderate

FORT CALGARY HISTORIC SITE ✪✪

Calgary began life as a wooden stockade built in six weeks by the North West Mounted Police in 1875 to curb the lawlessness of the illicit whiskey trade spilling over the US border. It's long since gone, and what you see today is a reconstruction of the first fort on the original site, set in lovely parkland. You can watch history unfold as the fort and its interpretive center recall the daily lives of the people of Calgary from 1875 to 1940, using a mixture of evocative photographs, dynamic exhibits, written documents and interactive interpretation. The site includes a replica of the 1888 barracks, and close by is Hunt House (not open) and Deane House, built in 1906 by Superintendent Deane, the local head of the Mounties.

GLENBOW MUSEUM ✪✪✪

The Glenbow is one of western Canada's finest museums, home to an impressive collection of over a million artifacts, photographs and works of art. Bright, modern and well-designed, its outstanding art, historical displays and First Nations exhibits provide the perfect introduction to the area, using a variety of media – film, music, sound, dance, sculpture and hands-on displays. The latest addition, The Blackfoot Gallery – Nitsitapiisinni: Our Way of Life, focuses on the history of the Blackfoot people, highlighting all aspects of their lives, culture, art and their suffering following the arrival of European settlers. Other galleries illustrate the history of the Inuit and the mixed-race French-speaking Métis, the Riel Uprising, the fur trade, the North West Mounted Police and the development of the oil and gas industries. Art in Asia is also featured, with a superb collection of sacred Buddhist and Hindu artifacts. Many of the museum's exhibits were bequeathed by Eric Harvie, a lawyer, oilman and rancher. He also had a passion for mineralogy and left an outstanding collection of gems, stones and minerals, including some very rare examples.

www.glenbow.org
✉ 130 9th Avenue SE
☎ 403/268-4100
🕐 Museum: daily 9–5 (also 5–9pm Thu). Library: Tue–Fri 10–5
🍴 Lazy Loaf and Kettle Café outside the entrance ($–$$)
♿ Good
✋ Moderate

HERITAGE PARK HISTORICAL VILLAGE ✪✪

Canada's largest living historic village re-creates the sights and sounds of life in Calgary at the turn of the 20th century. Set in 27ha (67 acres) of lush parkland in the heart of Calgary, the village features more than 150 buildings and exhibits with costumed guides in attendance. You can visit the SS *Moyie* sternwheeler and cruise the reservoir, board an authentic steam locomotive, ride around town in a horse-drawn carriage, enjoy the thrills of an antique midway (funfair) or take a stroll down Main Street (circa 1910), lined with stores and saloons. Your entrance fee also entitles you to a free western-style breakfast between 9 and 10am throughout the summer.

www.heritagepark.ca
✉ 1900 Heritage Drive SW
☎ 403/268-8500
🕐 Daily 9–5, mid-May to early Sep; Sat–Sun 9–5, early Sep–Oct
🍴 Choice in park ($–$$)
♿ Good ✋ Expensive

Above: *First Nations clothing and jewelry on display at the Glenbow Museum*

PRINCE'S ISLAND PARK ✪✪

Peaceful Prince's Park Island, set on an artificial island in the middle of the Bow River, offers a welcome respite from sightseeing, just minutes from downtown Calgary. Lying opposite the colorful Eau Claire Market and accessed by several bridges, this urban oasis of green and shady nooks is free from traffic and is a favorite haven for locals and visitors. The formal gardens and lawns are particularly pleasant in spring and summer and are perfect for a stroll or a picnic (tables are provided). One of Calgary's finest restaurants, the River Café (➤ 98), is located on the island.

✉ In the Bow River, north of Eau Claire Market
🍴 River Café (➤ 98)
♿ Good

Food & Drink

Some of the best ingredients in Canada are found in the west, from Pacific and Arctic seafood to Alberta beef and the fruits and wines of the Okanagan Valley. In the top city restaurants, they are used in exciting fusion cuisine.

First Nations Food

The Europe-size chunk of land between Canada's Great Lakes and the Rocky Mountains has never been particularly friendly territory for vegetarians. Even before the first Europeans started arriving in the mid-19th century, bringing their cattle with them, protein in all its fleshy forms dominated the diets of the First Nations tribes who wandered across the region in search of food. They caught fish, of course – trout, grayling, char, muskellunge, sturgeon and whitefish, primarily from the 200,000sq km (77,220sq miles) of lakes in Manitoba and northern Saskatchewan. But most of them depended for survival on the huge herds of bison that roamed the Prairies.

Elements of the aboriginal diet are still available on the Prairies. Freshwater fish are plentiful and Western chefs have devised all sorts of imaginative ways to serve them. Purists insist, however, that the old ways are still best – broiled or pan-fried with a side dish of wild rice and perhaps a dressing made with Saskatoon berries (a local delicacy that looks a lot like the blueberry).

Bison burgers and bison steaks are still available, as well, even though the great herds have shrunk to a tiny remnant of what they once were and most of the meat served today comes from farm-raised animals. The meat, however, is still lean and richly flavored. Other First Nations delicacies available are wild boar, caribou, moose, cornbread and bannock (a kind of flatbread cooked on a skillet).

Salmon berries have the color of the fish, but (thankfully) the taste of raspberries

Salmon are hung to dry beneath tipis at the First Nations fall camp at Lillooet

Prairies Specialties

The main source of protein these days is beef, and Alberta's ranches produce some of the best in the world – juicy, marbled and ready for the grill – and the West is for the most part unapologetic about its carnivorous appetites. Successive waves of immigrants have added their flavors to this meat-and-potatoes landscape. Ukrainians brought borscht, cabbage rolls and pirogis (little boiled dumplings stuffed with potatoes or cheese or vegetables); and Mennonite farmers from Germany adapted the sausages of home to local tastes, often by switching the emphasis from pork to beef.

Seafood and Freshwater Fish

Across the mountains, the whole culinary picture changes dramatically. What beef is to the Prairies, salmon is to British Columbia, and the region's chefs – heavily influenced by the new-wave cooking of California and Washington state across the border – serve filets glazed with Asian spices or raw as sushi or poached with pineapples. But one of the most popular ways to prepare it remains to cook it as the Pacific tribes did – barbecued on a soaked cedar plank. The West Coast fisheries provide more than just salmon, of course. Fresh sole, halibut, Alaskan king crab and its Dungeness cousin, Fanny Bay oysters, clams and ling cod are among the bounty that appear regularly on local menus and in local markets.

North of 60 in Yukon and the Northwest Territories, the range of local delicacies narrows considerably, but the fish is marvelous. Trout from cold mountain lakes are particularly sweet and a well-cooked and fresh Arctic char makes salmon taste almost pedestrian by comparison.

Top: Okanagan Valley vineyards produce some quality wines
Above: shopping at Vancouver's Stevenston Fish Market

Fresh salmon steaks are just one of the treats on offer at the Granville Island market

Calgary Stampede

Come to Calgary in July and you'll witness one of Canada's most spectacular events. The Calgary Stampede bills itself at "The Greatest Outdoor Show on Earth" and for ten days every year a million visitors from around the world come to watch events that include North America's biggest, richest and most dangerous rodeo. It all began in 1912 when rodeo entertainer Guy Weadick offered a jackpot of $16,000 – a fortune in those days – to attract competitors. Today the prize money amounts to around $600,000.

Start your day with a traditional breakfast of bacon and flapjacks, before heading off to Stampede Park, just south of downtown at 1410 Olympic Way SE, where most of the action takes place. Events include roping calves, wrestling steers, riding buffalo and bulls, lassoing and staying on a bucking bronco and the world-famous chuck wagon races, the most popular in terms of sheer spectacle and danger. It's an awesome sight as the teams, each consisting of a driver, four horses and four outriders, their wagons loaded with tent poles and a stove, fly round a figure-eight course, then along the 800-m (2,625-ft) main track.

A giant midway (funfair), casino and concerts provide additional entertainment, but the highlight is the Stampede Parade that kicks off the event. Some 150 floats, marching bands, 700 horses and 4,000 participants, including the Stampede Queen and Princesses, march past in front of the spectators who gather along the 5-km (3-mile) route.

If you plan to visit the city during the Stampede make reservations for accommodations and get tickets for the main events well in advance – they sell like hot cakes. Contact **www**.calgary-stampede.com for further details.

Chuckwagon racing is one of the most exciting events at the Calgary Stampede

What to See in the Prairies

BATOCHE NATIONAL HISTORIC SITE ✪

It was at Batoche that the Métis, of mixed French and First Nations blood, settled in the 19th century after leaving Red River in Manitoba, but their hope to pursue their traditional way of life in peace were not to be realized. Louis Riel, their charismatic leader, selected the site, strategically overlooking the South Saskatchewan River, as his headquarters and it became the last battlefield in the 1885 rebellion over land titles.

Several original buildings have been restored at the Batoche National Historic Site, including the church, rectory and the cemetery, which contains the graves of the guerilla leader Gabriel Dumont, who commanded the last stand, Batoche founder Xavier Letendre and the Métis who were killed in the final assault. The displays and audio-visual presentations at the visitor center are excellent, and the helpful costumed staff is on hand to explain more.

www.pc.gc.ca/lhn-nhs/sk/batoche
🔲 60 C2
✉ Rosthern, Saskatchewan
☎ 306/423-6227
🕐 Daily 9–5, early May–Sep
🍴 Snack concessions ($)
♿ Visitor center: good. Trails flat, but cemetery has no paved walkways
👍 Moderate

CARDSTON ✪

The little town of Cardston lies in the foothills of the Rocky Mountains, just a half hour from Waterton Lakes National Park (▶ 45). It is famous for having the largest Mormon tabernacle outside the USA (grounds only open), and for its fine carriage museum, one of the largest in North America. Located in 8ha (20 acres) of parkland in the beautiful Lee Creek Valley, the **Remington-Alberta Carriage Centre** has a superb collection of some 250 horse-drawn vehicles. These range from simple buggies and utility wagons to elegant carriages used by royalty and the stagecoaches of the Old West. You can tour the tack room, workshop, stables and corrals, watch skilled craftsmen restore the carriages and meet the horses that pull them.

www.town.cardston.ab.ca
🔲 60 A1
Remington-Alberta Carriage Centre
✉ 623 Main Street, Cardston, Alberta
☎ 403/653-5139
🕐 Daily 9–8, mid-May to mid-Sep; 10–5, rest of year
🍴 Cafés in town ($)
👍 Moderate

DID YOU KNOW?

The actress Fay Wray, who died in 2004, was born near Cardston in 1907. She made her name in the 1933 film *King Kong* – who can forget her screaming from the top of the Empire State Building?

Above: *a poignant reminder of a turbulent past – the Métis cemetery and simple little church at the Batoche National Historic Site*

CHURCHILL

www.pc.gc.ca/lhn-nhs/mb/prince

61 F5

Parks Canada Visitor Reception Centre

Bayport Plaza, Churchill, Manitoba

204/675-8863

Choice in town ($–$$$)

This monument in Cypress Hills commemorates the days of the early settlers

Remote Churchill stands on the southwestern shore of Hudson's Bay, at the mouth of the Churchill River, and for several months of the year is an ice-free port, but it is best known as the "Polar Bear Capital of the World." Late autumn is the best time to see the magnificent creatures, just before the bay refreezes. It's also a great place to see abundant bird life, whales, caribou and seals, and tours are available by helicopter, boat or "tundra buggy." Churchill is also a prime spot for observing the Northern Lights.

The Eskimo Museum in Vérendrye Street (closed Sun) has a vast range of tools, artifacts and carvings that focus on the lifestyle and history of the Inuit. Fort Prince of Wales lies across the estuary from Churchill. It was built by the Hudson's Bay Company between 1731 and 1771, and you can visit its bulwarks, barracks and commander's quarters on a guided boat tour (daily, Jul–Aug). Remember to bring insect repellent – the air teems with insects, especially mosquitoes.

Churchill is not accessible by road – there are scheduled flights and a rail service from Winnipeg, and the two-day journey across the tundra is one of Canada's more fascinating train rides. From late June to early August the ground is a glorious carpet of miniature flowers, including several species of cold-tolerant orchids.

CYPRESS HILLS AND FORT WALSH

www.cypresshills.com

60 B1

Cypress Hills

27km (17 miles) south of Maple Creek, Saskatchewan

306/662-5411 (Saskatchrewan); 403/893-3777 (Alberta)

Day pass: moderate

www.pc.gc.ca/lhn-nhs/sk/walsh

60 B1

Fort Walsh

Box 278, Maple Creek, Saskatchewan

306/662-2645

Daily, mid-May to early Sep

Limited

Moderate

The Blackfoot called the Cypress Hills area Ketewius Netumoo – "the hills that shouldn't be." They straddle the border between Alberta and Saskatchewan, and at more than 1,463m (4,800ft) are the highest point between the Rocky Mountains and Labrador, on the east coast.

Cypress Hills Interprovincial Park, the first of its kind in Canada, is a haven of peaceful lodgepole pine forests and rare wild flowers, high forested hills, panoramic views and quiet valleys, and is also home to many native animals such as wapiti (elk), deer, moose and trumpeter swans.

Fort Walsh National Historic Site, accessible from Cypress Hills or Maple Creek (on Highway 271), was a major North West Mounted Police post in the 1880s, and after the force became the Royal Canadian Mounted Police in 1920 it was their horse-breeding center. It has now been reconstructed, with interpretive displays covering the fort's history, the culture of the local First Nations people and background on the North West Mounted Police. **Farwell's Trading Post** nearby takes you back to the wild days of the illegal whiskey trade in Canada.

Cypress Hills Interprovincial Park

Leave Elkwater along the lakeside past the Visitor Information Centre and take the road signposted Ferguson Hill. At the next crossroads go right to Horseshoe Canyon. Head back to the intersection and go straight ahead, then across Route 41 (signposted Elkwater left and the US border right). Follow signs for Reesor Lake.

Much of the 18km (11 miles) to Reesor Lake is a plateau of thick grassland. Look for signs for Bull Trail, a passing point of wagon trains that once plied a north–south route, and the turning left for Spruce Coulee. The overview of Reesor Lake is on the right after 14km (8.5 miles). The road then sweeps on around the main body of the lake.

At the western lake head the asphalt gives way to dirt road. Turn left, signposted Fort Walsh.

Fort Walsh is right at a T-junction. Immediately to the right after the junction is a monument to Constable Graburn of the North West Mounted Police, the first officer to be killed in the line of duty (on November 12, 1879).

Make another left at the next T-junction and after 1.6km (1 mile) enter Saskatchewan. Cross the bridge at Battle Creek. There's a ranger station on the right half-way up the hill. About 14km (8.5 miles) after the border, go right on a tarmac road; it's 4km (2.5 miles) to Fort Walsh.

Fort Walsh (► opposite), just off the main route, offers a wonderful insight into Canadian history.

Return to the main route and turn right in the direction of Maple Creek. At the next T-junction, turn left; watch for a turning to the right, signed GAP Road, (a green sign states "Cypress Hills Road") approaching the other way. The GAP road turning is 9km (5.5 miles) from Fort Walsh.

This 22.5-km (14-mile) strip of land is a good place to see low-growing wild flowers in spring and summer.

At the end of GAP Road turn right to Loch Leven.

Distance 140km (87 miles)

Time 3 hours

Start point
Elkwater ➕ 60 B1

End point
Loch Leven ➕ 60 B1

Refreshments
Elkwater, Loch Leven, Fort Walsh (in season)

Warning:
It's not advisable to drive the route after prolonged wet weather as the dirt road section turns into a quagmire.

Beautiful Loch Leven Lake, in Cypress Hills Interprovincial Park

www.cd.gov.ab.ca/parks/
dinosaur
✚ 60 B2
✉ 48km (30 miles)
northeast of TransCanada
1 from Brooks, Alberta
☎ 403/378-4342
🕐 Daily
🍴 Dinosaur Service Centre
for snacks ($)
♿ Good
🎟 Free. Bus tours and
hikes: moderate

DINOSAUR PROVINCIAL PARK ✪✪

Dinosaur Provincial Park was created in 1955 to protect one of the world's most extensive dinosaur fields. Over 300 complete skeletons from 37 different species have been excavated, and new ones are unearthed nearly every year. Scientists now believe that some of the dinosaurs were carried here from farther north by glacial meltwaters and are not actually native to the area.

Much of the park is accessible only by a guided bus tour or hike. The popular bus tours give an excellent view of the Badlands landscape and take you to parts of the park that would otherwise be out of bounds to visitors (call for the latest schedules and to reserve a place). The park is also the site of a field station for the Royal Tyrrell Museum (➤ 25), and you can get a better idea of what goes on here by talking to the laboratory technicians who treat the skeletons after they have been excavated.

www.canadianbadlands.com
www.dinosaurvalley.com
✚ 60 B2
ℹ Drumheller Tourism
✉ 60 1st Avenue W,
Drumheller, Alberta
☎ 403/823-8100, 866/823-
8100 (toll-free in North
America)

DRUMHELLER AND THE ALBERTA BADLANDS ✪✪✪

The little town of Drumheller sits in the valley of the Red Deer River at the heart of the Alberta Badlands. This strange, otherwordly landscape of barren, sunbeaten hills, mud gullies, windblown bluffs and mushroom-shaped hoodoos was created by the action of wind, rain and glacial meltwater during the last Ice Age. The swamplands of Alberta were a haven for living dinosaurs and today this region is one of the world's most abundant sources of dinosaur fossils. (Some 96km/60 miles southeast of Drumheller is the Dinosaur Provincial Park, ➤ above.)

Drumheller is a good place to pick up the Dinosaur Trail, a 48-km (30-mile) circular route that links several historic sights and numerous viewpoints. Major attractions along the way are the world-famous Royal Tyrrell Museum of Palaeontology (➤ 25) and Horsethief Canyon – Canada's mini Grand Canyon – with its stunning multi-layered walls.

*Weird rock formations
(hoodoos) in the Badlands*

The Hoodoo Trail, 24km (15 miles) southeast of Drumheller on Highway 10 takes you past some of the most bizarre natural rock formations, known as hoodoos. Erosion has worn away the soft sandstone, leaving these strange, mushroom-shaped pillars, topped by caps of hard rock.

EDMONTON ✪✪

Edmonton, gateway to the unspoiled north, developed around a Hudson's Bay Company post called Edmonton House. In 1905 it became provincial capital, and the discovery of oil in the region in 1947 gave the city and the whole of Alberta a huge economic boost.

Downtown Edmonton is the most attractive part of the city; its ranks of granite and steel skyscrapers fill a tight grid on Jasper Avenue, the main street. At its heart is Churchill Square, dominated by modern buildings. These include City Hall, an interesting building that combines modern architecture with elements from the old City Hall, and the Citadel Theatre, the largest theater complex in Canada. Also here is the **Edmonton Art Gallery**, one of Alberta's oldest cultural institutions, containing over 5,000 historical and contemporary paintings, sculptures, prints, installation works and photographs from Canadian and international artists, with a strong focus on Alberta art.

West of downtown is the massive beaux-arts **Alberta Legislature Building**. This imposing 1913 structure stands in 23ha (57 acres) of parkland and is a must-see for anyone interest in architecture, politics and history. South of the river is the **Muttart Conservatory** (1977), a dramatic addition to the Edmonton townscape. Housing a spectacular display of plants, its glass pyramids have earned it the nickname "Giza on the Saskatchewan."

Don't miss a visit to the world's largest shopping and entertainment center, **West Edmonton Mall**, 15 minutes from downtown. In addition to more than 800 stores, attractions include Galaxyland, the world's largest indoor amusement park; World Waterpark, with swimming pools, slides, a wave pool and a bungee jump; Deep Sea Adventure with real submarine rides; daily dolphin presentations in Dolphin Lagoon; a roller coaster and a tropical rain forest.

www.edmonton.com
🚩 60 B3
ℹ️ Edmonton Tourism
✉️ Gateway Park, Gateway Boulevard (Highway 2)
☎️ 780/426-4715, 800/463/4667 (toll-free in North America)

www.edmontonartgallery.com
Edmonton Art Gallery
✉️ Sir Winston Churchill Square
☎️ 780/422-6223
🕐 Tue–Fri 10.30–5 (also 5–8pm Thu), Sat, Sun 11–5. Closed Mon
♿ Moderate

www.assembly.ab.ca/visitor
Alberta Legislative Building
✉️ 98th Avenue and 107 Street
☎️ 780/427-7362
🕐 Mon–Fri 8.30–5, Sat–Sun 9–5, May to mid-Oct; Mon–Fri 9–4.30, Sat–Sun noon–5, rest of year.
♿ Free

www.edmonton.ca/muttart
Muttart Conservatory
✉️ 9626–96A Street
☎️ 780/496-8755
🕐 Mon–Fri 9–5.30, Sat–Sun and holidays 11–5.30
♿ Moderate

www.westedmontonmall.com
West Edmonton Mall
✉️ 8882 170 Street
☎️ 780/444-5200
🕐 Mon–Fri 10–9, Sat 10–6, Sun noon–6. Hours vary for non-retail attractions
🍴 More than 100 dining options ($–$$$)

Glass pyramids of the Muttart Conservatory

HEAD-SMASHED-IN BUFFALO JUMP ✪✪

www.head-smashed-in.com
✚ 60 A1
✉ Highway 785 off Highway 2, 18 km (11 miles) NW of Fort MacLeod, Alberta
☎ 403/553-2731
🕐 Daily 9–6, mid-May to mid-Sep; 10–5, rest of year
🍴 Café ($) ♿ Good
🎟 Moderate

Head-Smashed-In is one of the best-preserved buffalo jumps in North America, designated a UNESCO World Heritage Site in 1981. For over 5,500 years the native people of the plains used it to kill the buffalo that provided them with food, hides for shelter and clothing, and bones and horns to make tools. A multi-million-dollar interpretive center, built into the cliff, tells the story of the people and explains the whole process.

The buffalo would be panicked into a stampede then forced to follow a path that ended at a cliff. The animals simply ran off the edge and fell to their death, to be butchered in a camp at the base of the cliff. Only enough buffalo were killed to provide the tribe with what they actually needed. Below the cliff an accumulation of bones and ash from those times lies more than 9m (30ft) deep.

The site includes trails, viewpoints, dioramas, artifacts and an 80-seat theater that shows a short film recreating a buffalo hunt.

REGINA ✪

www.tourismregina.com
✚ 61 D1
ℹ Tourism Regina
✉ PO Box 3335, Regina, Saskatchewan
☎ 306/789-5099, 800/661-5099

www.rcmpmuseum.com
RCMP Training Academy
✉ Dewdney Avenue W
☎ 306/780-5838
🕐 Museum daily, 8–6.45, mid-May to early Sep; 10–4.45, rest of year. Sergeant Major's Drill Mon, Wed, Fri 12.45pm, mid-May to Aug
🎟 Free, but donations accepted

Above: *Dioramas depict wildlife and hunting methods at Head-Smashed-In Buffalo Jump*

Regina grew from a small settlement called Pile o' Bones (after the buffalo bones left by First Nations hunters) into a cosmopolitan city and capital of Saskatchewan. It lies halfway between Winnipeg and Calgary in the heart of Canada's "breadbasket."

The North West Mounted Police (later the Royal Canadian Mounted Police) established their headquarters here in the 1880s and though this has since moved to Ottawa, the city has maintained its long association with the force. All Mounties do their basic training at the **RCMP Training Academy**, 4km (2.5 miles) west of the center, and their colorful graduation ceremonies are a highlight of a trip to Saskatchewan. You can watch horses and riders perform at the Sergeant Major's Drill.

The small downtown area has little to offer visitors, but south of here is Wascana Park, the city's main recreation area, with a bandstand, barbecue pits, snack bars, and boating and waterfowl ponds. This beautiful urban park is also home to the Saskatchewan Science Centre, the Royal Saskatchewan Museum, the Saskatchewan Centre of Arts, the Mackenzie Art Gallery and the Legislative Building, with its impressive 57-m (187-ft) dome.

RIDING MOUNTAIN NATIONAL PARK ✪✪

Riding Mountain National Park rises dramatically from the surrounding prairie landscape and is part of the upland known as the Manitoba Escarpment. Its 2,966sq km (1,145sq miles) of rolling hills incorporate three very different landscapes – deciduous forest to the east, boreal forest to the north and aspen parkland in the west – and is home to a variety of wildlife, such as wolves, moose, elk, lynx, beavers, bears and bison.

Wasagaming, the main town, sits on Clear Lake, the largest body of water in the park. Its crystal waters are ideal for scuba diving, sailing and fishing for perch, pike and trout. With over 400km (250 miles) of trails and opportunities for downhill skiing at Agassiz Ski Hill, the park is a year-round playground. A visit to the First Nations Anishinabe Village gives a picture of life here before European settlement.

www.pc.gc.ca/pn-np/mb/riding
🗺 61 E1
ℹ Wasagaming, Manitoba
☎ 204/848-7275
🕐 Visitor Centre: daily 9.30–8, late Jun–Aug; 9–5.30, mid-May to late Jun and Sep to mid-Oct
🚌 Grey Goose Bus Lines (summer only) to Wasagaming
🍴 Refreshments at Wasagaming and Lake Audy ($–$$)
♿ Good
👆 Inexpensive

ROYAL TYRREL MUSEUM, DRUMHELLER (► 25, TOP TEN)

First Nations heritage is on display at Saskatoon's Wanuskewin Heritage Centre

SASKATOON ✪

In a fine setting on the banks of the South Saskatchewan River, Saskatoon was founded in 1883, though for some 8,000 years it had been inhabited by First Nations people. Their history can be explored at the **Wanuskewin Heritage Centre**, 5km (3 miles) to the north via Highway 11.

A small township developed here after the Canadian Pacific Railway brought settlers as far as Regina by rail, and railroad history is recalled at the 3-ha (7.5-acre) **Saskatchewan Railway Museum**, which includes rides on working stock. Another attraction is the **Western Development Museum**, which has displays relating to the history of the province and the European settlement of the Prairies. This included a strong Ukrainian community, and the city is home to one of the country's premier collections of Ukrainian art and artifacts.

www.tourismsaskatoon.com
🗺 60 C2
ℹ Tourism Saskatoon
✉ 6-350 Idylwyld Drive N
☎ 306/242-1206

www.wanuskewin.com
Wanuskewin Heritage Centre
✉ Wanuskewin Road (RR4)
☎ 306/931-6767
🕐 Tue–Sun 9–5 Apr–Dec
👆 Inexpensive

www.saskrailmuseum.org
Saskatchewan Railway Museum
✉ RR3 via highways 7 and 60
☎ 306/382-9855
🕐 Daily 1–6, Jun–Aug; Sat–Sun 1–6, Sep
👆 Inexpensive

www.wdm.ca
Western Development Museum
✉ 2610 Lorne Avenue S
☎ 306/931-1910
🕐 Tue–Sun 9–5, Apr–Dec
👆 Inexpensive

DID YOU KNOW?

If you ever have a close encounter with a bear don't: scream, run away, make sudden movements, make direct eye contact or climb a tree – black bears can climb them too.

The North

In 1999, the former Northwest Territories (NWT) were split in two. The eastern section became the territory of Nunavut (Inuit for "our land") and its capital (formerly Frobisher Bay) became Iqaluit. Covering almost a fifth of Canada, bounded to the south by Manitoba, it appears to be a frozen wasteland, but come spring it bursts into life and a beautiful patchwork of colorful flowers covers the land. Together with the Yukon, these territories make up around 40 percent of Canada's land mass. Although the subarctic region has a handful of cities, nature dominates, and north of the Arctic Circle remains virtually uninhabited.

The Yukon will forever be associated with the Klondike Gold Rush, and the highways that cross it make it the easiest of the three territories to get around. The NWT has fewer roads, but has two of the largest lakes in the world and is one of the world's last great wilderness refuges.

' There's a land where the mountains are nameless,
And the rivers all run God knows where;
There are lives that are erring and aimless,
And deaths that just hang by a hair;
There are hardships that nobody reckons;
There are valleys unpeopled and still;
There's a land – oh, it beckons and beckons,
And I want to go back – and I will '

ROBERT SERVICE ("The Spell of the Yukon")
Songs of a Sourdough (1907)

Dawson City

Dawson City grew out of a marshy swamp near the confluence of the Klondike and Yukon rivers following the discovery of gold at Bonanza Creek in 1896. It became one of the most famous places on earth, but just three years later the rush came to an end and the prospectors were lured west to Alaska by news of a new strike at Nome, leaving Dawson to decline.

In 1953 the Yukon's first capital surrendered its role to Whitehorse, but a public campaign to preserve this important piece of Canada's history saw an upturn in Dawson's fortunes and today more than 30 buildings have been restored.

Each summer the population swells as visitors come to sample the Dawson experience and soak up the atmosphere of days gone by, meandering the boardwalks and visiting national historic treasures; touring the Klondike Gold Fields and trying their luck panning for gold. The epicenters of the Gold Rush – Bonanza and Eldorado creeks – lie 19km (12 miles) from Dawson, and both make fascinating excursions.

This tumbledown cabin once housed a hopeful 19th-century gold miner

What to See in Dawson City

DAWSON CITY MUSEUM ✪✪

To place Dawson's restored buildings in their historical context pay a visit to the city museum, housed in a 1901 neoclassical building. Its three main galleries feature many exhibits on the Gold Rush era, including evocative photographs that highlight the difficult conditions in which the miners lived and worked, an early silent film that came to light in 1978 during a restoration project, and a reconstruction of the old Dawson City Courthouse.

Minto Park; next to the museum, has a collection of old locomotives and machinery from the Klondike's early mining operations.

www.dawsoncity.org
⊞ 82 A4
ℹ Tourism Yukon Visitor Reception Centre and Klondike Visitors Association
✉ Corner of Front and King streets
☎ 867/993-5566, 877/465-3006 (toll free)
🕐 Daily 8–8, mid-May to late Sep

www.dawsoncity.org
✉ 5th Avenue
☎ 867/993-5291
🕐 Daily 10–6, late May–Labour Day
🍽 Café ($)
♿ Moderate

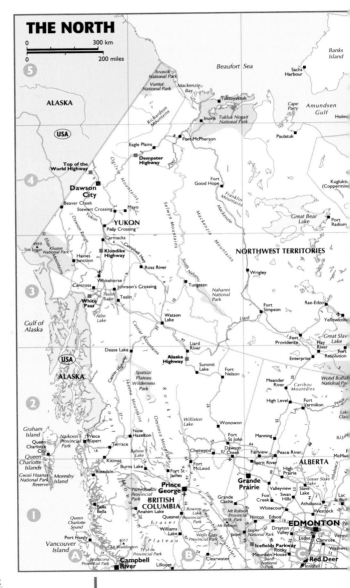

THE NORTH

0   300 km
0   200 miles

ALASKA

USA

Banks Island

Sachs Harbour

Beaufort Sea

Ivvavik National Park

Vuntut National Park

Mackenzie Bay

Tuktoyaktuk

Cape Parry

Amundsen Gulf

Holm

Inuvik

Tukluk Nogait National Park

Paulatuk

Richardson Mountains

Eagle Plains

Fort McPherson

Dempster Highway

Peel

Fort Good Hope

Franklin Mountains

Kugluktu (Coppermine

Top of the World Highway

Ogilvie Mountains

Dawson City

Beaver Creek

Mayo

Selwyn Mountains

Mackenzie

Great Bear Lake

Port Radium

Yukon

YUKON

Pelly Crossing

Carmacks

Campbell Hwy

NORTHWEST TERRITORIES

Dawson Range

4959 Mt Logan

Kluane National Park

Klondike Highway

Haines Junction

Ross River

South Nahanni

Wrigley

St Elias Mountains

Whitehorse

Johnson's Crossing

Tungsten

Nahanni National Park

Fort Simpson

Rae-Edzo

Carcross

White Pass

Teslin Lake

Teslin

Cassiar Mountains

Watson Lake

Liard

Yellowknife

Great Slav Lake

Atlin Lake

Gulf of Alaska

ALASKA

USA

Dease Lake

Liard River

Alaska Highway

Summit Lake

Fort Nelson

Fort Providence

Hay River

Enterprise

Fort Resolution

Spatsizi Plateau Wilderness Park

Skeena Mountains

Meander River

Caribou Mountains

Wood Buffa National Par

Graham Island

Queen Charlotte City

Naikoon Provincial Park

Prince Rupert

New Hazelton

Terrace

Williston Lake

Wonowon

High Level

Fort Vermilion

Peace

Lake Clai

Bi

Queen Charlotte Islands

Kitimat

Rabine Lake

Omineca Mountains

Fort St John

Manning

Fairview

Peace River

ALBERTA

McMu

Gwaii Haanas National Park Reserve

Moresby Island

Burns Lake

Fort McLeod

Chetwynd

Dawson Creek

Spirit River

High Prairie

Bella Coola

Fort St James

Grande Prairie

Valleyview

Lesser Slave Lake

Lac B Bich

Tweedsmuir Provincial Park

Prince George

Fox Creek

Swan Hills

Slave Lake

Athabasca

Westlock

Queen Charlotte Sound

Bella Bella

Anahim Lake

BRITISH COLUMBIA

Grande Cache

Mt Robson 3954 Park

Whitecourt

Hinton Edson

Drayton Valley

EDMONTON

Pe

Port Hardy

Quesnel

Bowron Lake Provincial Park

Mt Robson

Jasper

Leduc

Camrose

Vermi

Vancouver Island

4017 Mt Waddington

Williams Lake

Wells Gray Provincial Park

Jasper National Park

Banff National Park

Icefields Parkway

Rocky Mountain House

Red Deer

53

Wawir

Strathcona Provincial Park

Campbell River

Lilloet

Plateau

Fraser

Clearwater

Innisfail

Tf-yl-os Provincial Park

A   **B**   **C**

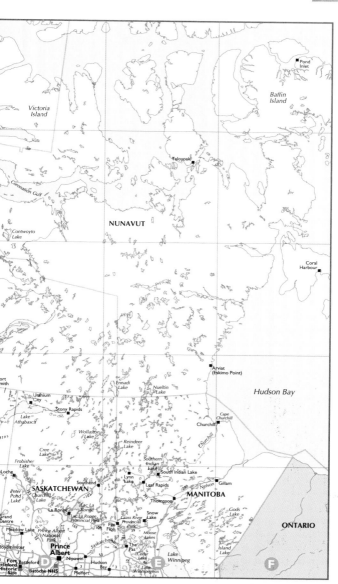

Pond Inlet

Baffin Island

Victoria Island

Coronation Gulf

Taloyoak

Contwoyto Lake

NUNAVUT

Coral Harbour

Fort Smith

Ennadi Lake

Nueltin Lake

Arviat (Eskimo Point)

Hudson Bay

Uranium City

Stony Rapids

Lake Athabasca

Wollaston Lake

Reindeer Lake

Cape Churchill

Churchill

Churchill

Cree Lake

Frobisher Lake

Loche

Southern Indian Lake

South Indian Lake

Gillam

Nelson

Peter Pond Lake

Churchill Lake

SASKATCHEWAN

Southend

Lynn Lake

Leaf Rapids

MANITOBA

Gods Lake

La Ronge

Lac La Ronge Provincial Park

Thompson

ONTARIO

Grand Centre

Meadow Lake

Prince Albert National Park

Grass River Provincial Park

Snow Lake

Flin Flon

Moose Lakes

Island Lake

Lloydminster

Prince Albert

Saskatchewan

The Pas

Cedar Lake

Lake Winnipeg

Fort Battleford Historic Site

Nipawin

Hudson Bay

Lake Winnipegosis

Batoche NHS

Melfort

✉ 8th Avenue, near Robert
Service's Cabin
🕐 Daily 10–6, mid-May to
mid-Sep
♿ Good
🎫 Inexpensive

JACK LONDON CABIN AND INTERPRETIVE CENTRE ✪

Born in San Francisco in 1876, Jack London came to the Klondike as a prospector in 1887, but like so many others he made no money. His experiences of life during those harsh days provided him with plenty of material for the books he later wrote. He depicted the Yukon and Alaska as an enticing, rugged, unspoiled area in his famous novel *Call of the Wild*. His tiny cabin at Stewart Crossing, south of town, has been re-created in Dawson City, and now contains an interpretive center illustrating his life, along with a small museum of memorabilia. Tours and readings of his works take place daily in summer.

✉ 8th Avenue
🕐 Daily 9–noon and 1–5,
mid-May to mid-Sep
♿ Good
🎫 Inexpensive

*The Robert Service cabin,
home of the popular poet*

ROBERT SERVICE'S CABIN ✪

A walking tour of Dawson City takes you past the cabin of the renowned English-born Canadian poet Robert Service (1874–1958). Here, the "Bard of the Yukon," author of *The Shooting of Dan McGrew* and *The Cremation of Sam McGee*, which he penned while living in Whitehorse, began full-time writing. The quaint little two-roomed cabin he rented contains its original woodstove, and stories and poetry recitals are offered daily in summer, along with tours of the site.

What to See in the North

ALASKA HIGHWAY ✪✪✪

Starting at "Mile Zero" in Dawson Creek (► 39), the Alaska Highway makes its way northward through British Columbia and across the border with the Yukon. It's an exciting excursion into some of the wildest landscapes in the world. Watson Lake (Mile 635) is the first town in the Yukon and the location of the unusual Signpost Forest, started when a homesick soldier stuck up a sign pointing to his hometown of Denville, Illinois. Since then some 10,000 people have followed suit.

From here the Highway heads westward, dipping back into British Columbia before it reaches Teslin (Mile 804). After rounding the lake here it continues west again to Whitehorse (► 89; Mile 918). At this point, many travelers switch to the Klondike Highway (► 86) and continue to Haines Junction.

www.themilepost.com
➕ 82 B2

BAFFIN ISLAND ✪

At nearly 500,000sq km (193,100sq miles), Baffin is the largest island in the Canadian Arctic and the fifth largest in the world (sixth if you count Australia). It forms the major part of Nunavut, Canada's newest territory, and **Iqaluit**, formerly Frobisher Bay, is its capital. With fewer than 10,000 people – mostly small Inuit groups – it is also one of the most sparsely populated areas in the world. Much of the island, a vast area of tundra, lies north of the Arctic Circle. This far north the summer is very short and there are only a few hours of sunlight a day in winter. The big attraction is the Inuit lifestyle and culture, along with opportunities for wildlife spotting (polar bears, whales, walruses), outdoor activities such as hiking, kayaking, canoeing, dogsledding and snowmobiling, and the chance to see the aurora borealis.

Baffin Island isn't the easiest of places to get to, or get around, but Iqaluit airport is a modern facility that doubles as an alternate landing site for the US space program. Several domestic Canadian airlines link the town with major Canadian centers. Just one highway links communities – the 26-km (16-mile) route between Arctic Bay and Nanisivik on the Borden Peninsula in the far north.

A fly-in trip to the 21,760-sq-km (8,400-sq-mile) **Auyuittuq National Park** on the island's Cumberland Peninsula is a must. The name means "the land that never melts." Hiking and climbing are popular activities in June and July when the snow *has* melted and the meadows are covered with clumps of tundra grasses.

www.nunavuttourism.com
➕ 83 F5
ℹ Nunavut Tourism, Box 1450, Iqaluit
☎ 867/979-6551, 866/686-2888 (toll-free in North America)
✈ Flights to Iqaluit from Yellowknife, Ottawa and Montréal

Auyuittuq National Park
✉ PO Box 353, Pangnirtung, NWT
☎ 867/473-8828
⛴ From Pangnirtung after ice melts in June

---

www.town.inuvik.nt.ca
www.inuvik.ca
✚ 82 B5
ℹ Western Arctic Visitor
   Centre, Mackenzie Road
☎ 867/777-8616
🚌 Twice-weekly Dawson
   City–Inuvik service
✈ Regular, from Yellowknife

INUVIK AND THE MACKENZIE RIVER ✪

Inuvik is the major settlement in the north of the Northwest Territories and makes an excellent base for exploring this vast Arctic region. It sits in the delta of the Mackenzie River, a wonderful freshwater environment. This lively town, with its multicolored homes raised above the permafrost, gives a cheerful splash of color to the otherwise barren wilderness. Look out for the circular **Church of Our Lady of Victory** on the Mackenzie Road, a

major landmark in the town. Painted white, it bears a striking resemblance to an igloo and is often referred to as the "igloo church." Inside you will find a series of paintings, *Stations of the Cross*, by local Inuit artist Mona Thresher. Each summer the town hosts the Great Northern Arts Festival, a ten-day gathering of artists and performers from across the Arctic and beyond.

You can charter a small plane to visit one of the national parks in the area – Ivvavik or Tuktut Nogait – where you can go hiking, kayaking and whitewater rafting, or view such wildlife as musk oxen, caribou and grizzly bears. In winter the chance to see the aurora borealis is a big draw. The Dempster Highway is the only road into Inuvik.

www.touryukon.com
✚ 82 A3
ℹ Tourist receptions at
   Whitehorse, Carmacks
   and Dawson City
☎ 867/456-7623 for 24-hour
   information on the road
🚌 Daily bus Whitehorse to
   Dawson City (May–Sep)
✈ Vancouver to Whitehorse

Above: *The skeleton of a mammoth is one of the intriguing displays at the Beringia Interpretive Centre, Whitehorse*

KLONDIKE HIGHWAY ✪✪

The Klondike Highway follows the route taken by prospectors during the Gold Rush in the 1890s. Disembarking at Skagway in Alaska, USA, they headed north on foot or horseback to Whitehorse and continued their journey by boat on the Yukon River to Dawson City.

Technically it starts at Skagway, but for many people the real Klondike Highway is the northern section between Whitehorse and Dawson City. North of Whitehorse endless banks of conifers carpet the slopes of the mountains. Carmacks, 190km (118 miles) from Whitehorse, is a First Nations village named after George Carmacks, who first discovered gold in the area. Twenty-two km (13.5 miles) farther you come to the halfway point at Five Fingers Rapids. The road then continues through Minto and Pelly Crossing to Stewart Crossing, location of Jack London's orginal cabin (▶ 84). The Silver Trail leads east from here, through the former silver mining towns of Mayo and Elsa to Keno, while the Klondike Highway continues to Dawson City, via Glenboyle. At Glenboyle the Dempster Highway heads northeast to Inuvik (▶ above).

King's Throne Trail

This is one of the most spectacular of the shorter trails in Kluane National Park.

Start at the trailhead left of the parking area as you look at the lake (watch out for the huge tree roots crisscrossing it). After 800m (2,625ft) the footpath skirts the lake on your right. Continue 350m (1,148ft) to where the route splits, and follow the King's Throne Trail signs left.

In the other direction, the Cottonwood Trail is one of the longest trails in the park, at 84km (52 miles). The King's Throne route climbs through woodland away from the lake.

At a second split in the trail, take the left fork and continue climbing. The path becomes a series of tight switchbacks and narrows to a single file, then breaks through the treeline, with a panoramic view north and Kathleen Lake in the foreground. Keep on climbing to the lip of the cirque, a rock bowl gouged out of the mountain peak by glacial action.

Admire the full spectacle of the Yukon countryside spread out far below, then explore the rock-strewn surface of the cirque, with its relatively smooth sides. From here you can hike along the ridge to the King's Throne summit, which offers stunning views to the west over some of the most typical Kluane landscape. This part of the trail is not marked as clearly as on the lower section, so extra care is needed.

Return to your car by retracing your route.

Distance
9.6km (6 miles)

Time
Allow 6 hours

Start/end point
Kathleen Lake parking area
✚ 82 A3

Lunch
Kluane Park Inn ($$)
✉ Haines Junction

The St. Elias Mountains form a jagged horizon beyond the scrubland of the Kluane National Park

KLUANE NATIONAL PARK

www.pc.gc.ca/pn-np/yk/kluane
82 A3
PO Box 5495, Haines Junction, Yukon
867/634-7250
Free; charge for camping

Haines Junction Visitor Centre
Daily, mid-May to mid-Sep; most weekdays rest of year

The Kaskawulsh Glacier is a feature of this typical Northern landscape

Kluane National Park covers more than 22,000sq km (8,494sq miles) in the southwestern corner of the Yukon and takes its name from the Tutchone First Nations word meaning "place of many fish." This breathtaking park includes the mighty St. Elias Range, which contains the highest peak in Canada – Mount Logan (6,048m/19,840ft) – and the world's largest non-polar icefields, a vast network of more than 4,000 glaciers. Most of the park is inaccessible wilderness – the best way to see the icefields and the mountains is to take a tour in a small plane – but the Alaska Highway between Whitehorse and Beaver Creek will give you spectacular views of the distant mountains.

The main center, Haines Junction, is an obvious staging point for outdoor activities, with excellent opportunities for hiking (► 87). At the visitor center here you can find out everything you need to know about the park.

About 74km (46 miles) west of Haines Junction is Kluane Lake, a vast, beautiful stretch of glacier-fed water, 60km (37 miles) long, where you can take to a boat and fish for Arctic char and trout.

NAHANNI NATIONAL PARK

www.pc.gc.ca/nahanni
82 B3
Nahanni National Park Reserve
Box 348, Fort Simpson
867/695-3151
Park: daily mid-Jun to mid-Sep. Office: daily 8–noon and 1–5, mid-Jun to mid-Sep; Mon–Fri 8.30–noon and 1–5, rest of year
Expensive

This unspoiled wilderness, in the southwest part of the NWT, is one of the most remote national parks in Canada. Within its boundaries is a section of the Mackenzie Mountains, with its high peaks, deep canyons, hot springs and waterfalls. The best way to see the park is to charter a small plane to Virginia Falls or Rabbitkettle Lake.

The spectacularly wild South Nahanni River is renowned as the world's premier whitewater rafting location, and Mount Wilson, at Moose Ponds, is a popular starting point for gentler canoe trips. Other highlights include the Tufa Mounds, 27-m (88.5-ft) high domes of soft calcium; the Ragged Range, where molten igneous rock has been thrust up and eroded into jagged peaks; Rabbitkettle Hot Springs, where the water is a constant 20°C (68°F); and Virginia Falls, at 92m (300ft) twice the height of Niagara Falls, with its downstream canyons.

The park is home to many species of animals, including Dall's sheep, mountain goats, caribou and bears (black and grizzly). For climbers who like a challenge there is the Cirque of the Unclimbables, with its sheer rocky peaks.

WHITEHORSE ⚫⚫

During the Gold Rush days of the 1890s, Whitehorse became an important town on the Klondike Highway from Skagway to Dawson City (➤ 86) as prospectors rested here before taking to the Yukon River for the last leg of their epic journey. The town really took off and developed when construction of the Alaska Highway (➤ 85) began in 1942, and it took over from Dawson City as capital of the Yukon in 1953. Today it is a lively town, and with the only major airport in the territory, it makes the perfect base for exploring the Yukon and the White Pass area. The **White Pass**, a steep, narrow ravine running southwest of Whitehorse to Skagway, Alaska, is one of the most dramatic routes in Canada and can be traveled by car or by the narrow-gauge railway.

Most people head first for the **SS Klondike**. This 1929 sternwheeler, now fully restored, used to travel the river between Whitehorse and Dawson City, carrying people and goods on the seven-day journey.

The **MacBride Museum**, in a charming log cabin on the scenic waterfront, gives a good account of the Yukon's past and Whitehorse's part in the Gold Rush, with a wonderful collection of photographs, archive material, Gold Rush memorabilia, a locomotive from the White Pass and Yukon Railroad, and First Nations and Northwest Mounted Police exhibits.

West of Whitehorse are **Takhini Hot Springs**, where you can relax in an outdoor pool in natural mineral water maintained at a temperature of around 38°C (100.4°F).

The SS Klondike

www.city.whitehorse.yk.ca
www.visitwhitehorse.com
🔲 82 A3
ℹ️ Whitehorse Visitor Reception Centre
✉️ 100 Hanson Street, Whitehorse, Yukon
☎️ 867/667-3084
✈️ From Calgary, Edmonton and Vancouver

SS Klondike
✉️ Docked: 300 Main Street
☎️ 867/667-3910
🕐 Daily, mid-May to mid-Sep
👆 Inexpensive

MacBride Museum
✉️ 1124 - 1st Avenue
☎️ 867/667-2709
🕐 Daily 10–7, mid-May to mid-Sep; noon–5 rest of year 👆 Inexpensive

YELLOWKNIFE ⚫

The capital of the Northwest Territories is the main base for exploring the north and the hub of many northern air routes. The heart of the city is the Old Town, along the shores of the Great Slave Lake, the perfect place for kayaking and canoeing or taking a summer cruise. Yellowknife is also a popular base for wildlife-viewing trips to see caribou and musk-ox herds, and for seeing the midnight sun and the aurora borealis.

The town originated as a prospectors' camp that grew up when gold was found in the region is 1934, but it's famous now for diamonds. The Diavik Diamond Mines lie 320km (200 miles) northwest, but there's a visitor center in their Yellowknife office on 50th Avenue.

The area is the ancestral home of the Dogrib Dene First Nations. Their history is the focus of the excellent **Prince of Wales Heritage Centre**, off the Ingraham Trail, west of New Town. It's the principal museum for the region.

www.northernfrontier.com
🔲 82 C3
ℹ️ Northern Frontier Visitor Centre
✉️ 4807 - 49th Street
☎️ 867/873-4262
🕐 Mon–Fri 8.30-6 (5.30 Sep–May), Sat–Sun and holidays noon–4

www.pwnhc.ca
Prince of Wales Heritage Centre
☎️ 867/873-0205
🕐 Daily 10.30–5.30, Jun–Aug; Mon–Fri 10.30–5, Sat–Sun noon–5, rest of year
👆 Free

The Golden Circle

Distance
483km (300 miles)

Time
2 days (not including time for hiking on park trails)

Start/end point
Whitehorse ➕ 82 A3

Refreshment
Antonio's Vineyard ($–$$)
✉ 202 Strickland Street, Whitehorse

Raven Hotel ($$)
✉ Haines Junction

www.skagway.org
ℹ Skagway Convention and Visitors Bureau
☎ 907/983-2854

www.haines.ak.us
ℹ Haines Convention and Visitors Bureau
☎ 907/766-2234

Warning:
Distances between settlements are great. Keep an eye on your fuel at all times and plan ahead where you will stop for the night. Bring your passport and necessary documentation for the crossing into the USA. Note: Alaska is one hour ahead of Pacific Standard Time.

Traffic hold-ups are never an issue in this part of the world

This spectacular drive passes through some of the most pristine landscape in North America, taking you across the border into Alaska, USA.

Leave Whitehorse on 4th Avenue and Two Mile Hill to Route 1, the Alaska Highway (➤ 85), heading northwest to Haines Junction.

As you get close to Haines Junction the mighty peaks of Kluane National Park (➤ 88) appear directly ahead.

After 160km (100 miles), at Haines Junction, take the Haines Highway south to Haines City.

Some 27km (17 miles) south of Haines Junction turn right to Kathleen Lake, a popular spot for hiking and camping.

Continue past Dezadeash Lake to Kukshu, a traditional First Nations autumn camp. Around 90km (56 miles) from Haines Junction you'll cross into British Columbia.

The views are dominated by the St. Elias Mountains to the right. The road leads to the Chilkat Pass (145km/90 miles), the highest on this highway at 1,065m (3,461ft).

After 178km (110.5 miles) you'll cross into Alaska, USA (customs post open 7am–11pm Alaska Time). Head on to the Chilkat Bald Eagle Preserve, 32km (20 miles) away.

Thousands of eagles gather on the Chilkat Valley flats, especially in late autumn during the salmon spawning.

From here it's 35km (22 miles) to Haines City, a good place to stop overnight. Take the one-hour ferry ride from Haines City to Skagway, a quaint "Gold Rush" town. Follow the Klondike Highway north out of town and up to White Pass, 22km (13.5 miles) away. It's another 11km (7 miles) to the customs post (back in Canada).

North of Carcross is the Carcross Desert, the world's smallest at a little more than 1.6km (1 mile) long.

Where the Klondike Highway meets the Alaska Highway, it's 14km (8.5 miles) to Whitehorse.

Where To...

Above: *apple pie and cheese, a specialty of Vancouver's Raintree Restaurant*
Right: *First Nations artworks usually feature scenes of daily lifestyle and wildlife*

British Columbia & the Rockies

Prices

Approximate prices for a three-course meal for one person, including wine

$ = under $25
$$ = $25–$50
$$$ = more than $50

Diamond Ratings

As with the hotel ratings (▶ 100), AAA field inspectors evaluate restaurants on the overall quality of food, service, décor and ambiance – with extra emphasis given to food and service. Ratings range from one diamond (▼) indicating a simple, family-oriented place to eat to five diamonds (▼▼▼▼▼) indicating an establishment offering superb culinary skills and ultimate adult dining experience.

Banff, Alberta

Barbary Coast ($–$$)

Enjoy a drink and occasional live music at the bar or in the restaurant, which serves good steaks, salads, burgers, seafood, pastas and barbecued ribs.

www.banffbarbarycoast.com
⊠ Upper Level, 119 Banff Avenue ☎ 403/762-4616
◎ Daily 11.30am–2am

▼▼▼ Bistro Restaurant ($$–$$$)

The décor is simple and the food is French-inspired, but with Swiss (Röesti pizzas) and North American (steak, pasta, salmon, chowder) influences.

⊠ Wolf and Bear Mall, corner of Wolf and Bear streets
☎ 403/762-8900 ◎ Daily from 5pm

Evelyn's ($)

Evelyn's is one of the best cafés in Banff and is centrally located on the main street. The cakes, coffees, teas and snacks are all first-rate. A second Evelyn's, Evelyn's Too, can be found at 229 Bear Street (tel: 403/762-0330).

⊠ 201 Banff Avenue
☎ 403/762-0352 ◎ Mon–Sat 7am–11pm, Sun 7.30am–11pm

▼▼▼ Le Beaujolais ($$$)

The elegant interior is wood paneled, the tables covered in crisp white linen, and the food thoroughly French. You can eat à la carte, or choose from one of the set-price menus. There are 600 wines to choose from.

www.lebeaujolaisbanff.com
⊠ 212 Banff Avenue, corner of Buffalo Street ☎ 403/762-2712
◎ Daily 6–9.30pm

Melissa's ($$)

This is a local favorite, especially at lunchtime. The setting is memorable and the food, especially the steaks, excellent. Other dishes include trout, salmon and seafood, chicken, ribs, stews, pastas, burgers and pizzas. In summer you can eat or sip a beer on the outside deck.

⊠ 218 Lynx Street ☎ 403/762-5511 ◎ Daily 7am–9.45pm

Jasper, Alberta

Earl's ($–$$)

This casual dining place offers good standards such as burgers, pastas, and pizzas from a wood-burning oven. There are also more exotic dishes, influenced by the cuisines of Mexico, Europe and Asia.

⊠ 2nd Floor, 600 Patricia Avenue at Miette Avenue
☎ 780/852-2393 ◎ Daily from 11am

Mountain Foods ($)

This place may be more café than restaurant, but the food is varied, inexpensive, healthy and well-prepared (the menu changes regularly). You can also get snacks, soup, coffee or cakes, or buy food to take out

⊠ 606 Connaught Drive
☎ 780/852-4050 ◎ Daily 8am–10pm

Villa Caruso ($–$$)

Villa Caruso is a long-time favorite serving beef, seafood and pasta. Pizzas and other dishes are made in a wood-fired oven, and the steaks are cooked in dramatic, sizzling fashion in an open kitchen over a flame grill.

www.villacaruso.com
✉ 2nd Floor, 640 Connaught Drive ☎ 780/852-3920 ⌚ Daily 11am–midnight (3–11pm off season)

Kelowna, British Columbia

De Montreuil ($$)

Considered by many to be the finest restaurant in Kelowna, De Montreuil specializes in Cascadian cuisine (from the Cascade Mountain area). Try the buffalo tenderloin with lobster and morel fungi demiglace.
✉ 368 Bernard Avenue ☎ 250/860-5508 ⌚ Lunch 11–2, dinner from 5.30pm

Lake Louise, Alberta

Bill Peyto's Café ($)

A cafeteria-style eatery in the Lake Louise Youth Hostel. You don't have to be a guest at the hostel to enjoy the healthy, inexpensive and varied food. You can eat outdoors in good weather.
✉ Lake Louise Youth Hostel and Alpine Centre, 203 Village Road ☎ 403/522-2200 ⌚ Daily 8am–10pm (breakfast served until 2pm)

Station Restaurant at Lake Louise ($$–$$$)

Housed in the beautifully restored 1909 Lake Louise train station, there are also tables in vintage railroad dining cars. The food, mostly West Coast, includes herb-crusted salmon, burgers, Caesar salad, steaks and buffalo. There's a lounge bar and in good weather you can enjoy a barbecue in the station garden.
✉ 200 Sentinel Road ☎ 403/522-2600 ⌚ Daily 11.30am–midnight

Post Hotel ($$$)

The cuisine at the Post Hotel, one of the best restaurants in the Rockies, is a sophisticated fusion of European, Canadian, California and Asian cooking – Albertan beef, foie gras, English pea sauce, fresh scallops on jicama root, and red pepper and mango pineapple salsa with cilantro oil and jasmine rice all feature.
✉ 200 Pipestone Road ☎ 403/522-3989 ⌚ Daily 5–10pm

Vancouver, British Columbia

Bishop's ($$$)

The food at this popular venue is described as "contemporary home cooking" – a modern fusion of a range of cuisines such as Italian, French nouvelle cuisine, West Coast and Far Eastern. It's some distance from downtown, and you'll need to reserve well in advance.
✉ 2183 West 4th Avenue, near Yew Street ☎ 604/738-2025 ⌚ Dinner daily

Bridges ($–$$)

The best place for a sit-down brunch or lunch on Granville Island is Bridges, where you can tuck into nachos, pastas, fresh fish and seafood, and other North American staples. There's a lively pub and more formal dining area inside.
✉ 1696 Duranleau Street, Granville Island ☎ 604/687-4400 ⌚ Lunch and dinner daily

C ($$$)

Vancouver's best fish and seafood restaurant has a waterside setting with great views. The food is intense

Tipping

Tipping is far more prevalent in North America than Europe. All serving staff should be tipped, even in budget cafés and diners, unless service has been poor. Tip 15 percent or more of the check (bill) based on the total cost of the meal before taxes (► 98).

The Okanagan Wine Route

The Okanagan Valley owes much of its prosperity to fruit growing. Kelowna in particular grows a third of all Canada's apples, while the rest of the area produces the country's apricots, half its plums and 40 percent of its cherries and peaches. The area is also renowned for its wine, and many of Kelowna's orchards and vineyards offer guided tours. The wine route itself is well signed. Pick up a pamphlet at the local visitor information office.

and imaginative, with a heavy Asian influence – Arctic char or sea bass, for example, served with a rich wrap or noodles.
✉ **1600 Howe Street** ☎ **604/681-1164** Ⓖ **Lunch Mon–Fri, dinner daily**

CinCin ($$)

The food – rotisserie meat, fish and game – is predominantly Italian, but you can also eat paella and a wide variety of other dishes. The bar is open between meals for *antipasti* (appetizers) and pizza from the wood-fired oven. The pastries, bread and ice cream are all homemade.
✉ **1154 Robson Street, near Bute Street** ☎ **604/688-7338** Ⓖ **Lunch Mon–Fri, dinner daily**

Gallery Café ($)

The café at the Vancouver Art Gallery is a great place for coffee, lunch or snacks, whether or not you're visiting the gallery.
✉ **Vancouver Art Gallery, 750 Hornby Street** ☎ **604/688-2233** Ⓖ **Mon–Sat 9–5 (also Thu 5–9), Sun 10–5.30**

Hon's Wun Tun House ($)

Noodles are a specialty here, along with fried meat-filled dumplings and soups – you can choose from around 90. There's a take-out shop next door and other branches around the city, but this is the best.
✉ **268 Keefer Street, near Gore Street** ☎ **604/688-0871** Ⓖ **Lunch and dinner daily**

La Bodega ($$)

La Bodega is a long-established Spanish bar that's deservedly popular, so come early for a seat. Some

of the city's best tapas and fried chicken are served here, but many people just come to drink and chat.
✉ **1277 Howe Street, near Davie Street** ☎ **604/684-8814** Ⓖ **Mon–Fri 11.30am–midnight, Sat 5–midnight, Sun 5–11pm**

Le Crocodile ($$$)

Le Crocodile serves hearty French bistro dishes – steak tartare, beef tenderloin, rabbit, foie gras and rich desserts. It's a good place for a treat, and you don't have to go too far from downtown to enjoy it.
✉ **909 Burrard Street (entrance on Smithe Street)** ☎ **604/669-4298** Ⓖ **Lunch Mon–Fri, dinner Mon–Sat**

Lumière ($$$)

Two set-price, multicourse tasting menus nightly are a good way to sample the fabulous contemporary French cooking. Portions are small, so think again if you have a hearty appetite. The restaurant's some way from downtown.
✉ **2551 West Broadway, near Trafalgar Street** ☎ **604/739-8185** Ⓖ **Dinner Tue–Sun**

Naam ($)

Naam has a huge choice of vegetarian food – the french fries with miso gravy is a long-established classic – plus great desserts. On warm days you can eat out in the leafy courtyard. No reservations.
✉ **2724 West 4th Avenue, near Stephens Street** ☎ **604/738-7151** Ⓖ **Open daily 24 hours**

Old Spaghetti Factory ($)

The food here is simple but well prepared – pastas,

salads, steaks, chicken and the like. The atmosphere is informal, and lots of colored glass, plants, mirrors and antique memorabilia create a pleasant period ambience. It's located right in the heart of historic Gastown.

✉ **53 Water Street** ☎ **604/684-1288** ◉ **Lunch and dinner daily**

Pink Pearl ($$)

Pink Pearl offers an authentic Chinese dining experience. The cooking is mostly Cantonese, with great dim sum and seafood – make your choice from the tanks near the door which contain live lobsters, scallops, shrimp, oysters, rock cod and more.

✉ **1132 East Hastings Street, near Glen Street** ☎ **604/253-4316** ◉ **Lunch 9–3, dinner 5–10 (also 10–11pm Fri–Sat)**

▼▼▼ RainCity Grill ($$–$$$)

The menu at this popular restaurant changes almost by the week to take advantage of the best seasonal ingredients. The choice of wine and beer is good, especially wine by the glass.

✉ **1193 Denman Street, at Morton Street** ☎ **604/685-7337** ◉ **Dinner daily, also brunch Sat–Sun**

▼▼▼ Villa del Lupo ($$$)

Villa del Lupo is a wonderfully romantic place for a meal. One of the most famous dishes is the *osso buco* with cinnamon and other spices. The choice of Italian and California wines is first rate.

✉ **869 Hamilton Street, near Smithe Street** ☎ **604/688-7436** ◉ **Dinner daily**

▼▼ Water Street Café ($–$$)

On Gastown's main street near the famous steam clock, the Water Street Café has a pleasant patio for good weather (make a reservation to be sure of a place here, or by a window inside) and good, tasty, bistro-style food. At lunch you can choose from pastas, seafood (including great oysters), homemade focaccia and daily specials.

✉ **300 Water Street** ☎ **604/689-2832** ◉ **Lunch and dinner daily**

Yoho National Park, British Columbia

Emerald Lake Lodge ($$–$$$)

The Emerald Lake Lodge is by far the smartest hotel in the Yoho National Park and it includes a variety of cafés, bars and dining rooms to suit all budgets.

✉ **Emerald Lake Lodge, Emerald Lake, 8km (5 miles) north of Highway 1** ☎ **250/343-6321** ◉ **Daily**

▼▼ Kicking Horse Lodge and Café ($)

This is a good place to eat and stay in Field, the only settlement of any note in Yoho National Park. It's great for coffee and snacks, as well as full meals.

✉ **100 Centre Street, Field** ☎ **250/343-6303** ◉ **Daily 8–3, 5–9, late May–early Oct; Thu–Sat 5–9, mid-Dec to Mar**

▼ Truffle Pigs Café ($–$$)

All-day breakfasts, sandwiches and delicious baked goods are served at this funky café.

✉ **318 Stephen Avenue, Field** ☎ **250/343-6462** ◉ **Daily 8am–10pm (8.30–7 in winter)**

Dim Sum

For many Vancouverites, dim sum at one of the city's Chinese restaurants on Sunday lunchtime has become a ritual. Take a seat and jasmine tea or strong black Chinese *oolong* will be brought to your table. Then wait for the carts filled with steaming bamboo baskets of these tasty dumplings – savory and sweet – to be wheeled in your direction. Make your choice and when you finish, the waiter tots up the number of dishes on your table and presents your bill.

The Pacific Coast

Afternoon Tea

Taking English afternoon tea is something of a ritual in Victoria. The key places to go are the lounge of the Empress Hotel – about $30 a head – and the Blethering Place at 2250 Oak Bay Avenue. If you want tea, coffee, sandwiches and cakes in more ordinary surroundings, try Murchie's at 1110 Government Street (tel: 250/383-3112, open Mon–Sat 9–7, Sun 10–7).

Nanaimo, British Columbia
Mahle House ($)
The menu here changes weekly, but the food always uses the freshest local produce such as rabbit, chicken and venison, and is served in an intimate countryside setting.

⊠ **2104 Heemer Road**
☎ **250/722-3621** Ⓒ **Closed lunch and Mon–Tue**

Port Hardy, British Columbia
🍷 Stink Creek Café ($)
Don't be deterred by the name – there's excellent food on offer here. The lunch menu features homemade soups and sandwiches, and rhubarb muffins are a specialty.

⊠ **7030 Market Street**
☎ **250/949-8117** Ⓒ **Daily 5.30am–5pm. Closed major holidays**

Prince Rupert, British Columbia
Green Apple ($)
This shack is a local institution, renowned for its fresh halibut and fries.

⊠ **301 McBride Street**
☎ **250/627-1666** Ⓒ **Daily, times vary at the whim of the owner**

Qualicum Beach, British Columbia
🍷🍷 Old Dutch Inn ($$)
Servers dressed in Dutch costume add to the experience and there are wonderful sea views. In addition to world-famous pastries, there are Dutch specialties on the menu. Reservations are recommended in summer.

⊠ **2690 Island Highway**
☎ **250/752-1468** Ⓒ **Daily 4–10pm (closes 9pm Sun)**

Tofino, British Columbia
🍷🍷 🍷🍷 Pointe ($$$)
Jutting out into the ocean, this upscale restaurant has breathtaking views. Canadian West Coast cuisine features fresh seafood.

⊠ **Wickaninnish Inn, Osprey Lane/Chesterman Beach**
☎ **250/725-3100** Ⓒ **Daily, breakfast, lunch and dinner**

Victoria, British Columbia
Café Brio ($$–$$$)
The atmosphere is relaxed, the food predominantly Italian. Lunch is simple and inexpensive – pastas, salads and soups – but in the evening you can expect more adventurous dishes and slightly higher prices. A short taxi ride or 10-minute walk from downtown.

www.cafe-brio.com ⊠ **944 Fort Street** ☎ **250/383-0009** Ⓒ **Lunch and dinner daily**

🍷 Haultain Fish and Chip Café ($$)
Thanks to its strong British traditions, Victoria has a number of fish-and-chip restaurants. This is the best; the fish is always wonderfully fresh, and there's a take-out service.

⊠ **1127 Haultain** ☎ **250/383-8332** Ⓒ **Tue–Sat 11.30–8, Sun 3.30–7.30**

🍷🍷🍷 Herald Street Caffè ($$)
The cooking at this well-established restaurant is West Coast, with Italian leanings, generous portions and plenty of seasonal vegetables, meat, fish and seafood. Typical dishes might include crab cakes with pesto and salsa, a

lunchtime favorite. The wine list is exceptional.

✉ **546 Herald Street**
☎ **250/381-1441** Ⓒ **Lunch Wed–Sun, dinner daily**

🍷🍷 Il Terrazzo ($$)

The restaurant is popular with visitors and Victorians alike, who come for the good Italian food served in pretty, contemporary surroundings. Dishes range from reasonably priced small pizzas to more expensive main-course classics such as *scaloppini* and *osso buco*.

✉ **555 Johnson Street, off Waddington Alley** ☎ **250/361-0028** Ⓒ **Lunch and dinner daily**

🍷🍷 Keg Steakhouse ($$)

Overlooking the Inner Harbour, this restaurant serves the best steaks in the city, plus seafood dishes.

✉ **500 Fort Street** ☎ **250/386-7789** Ⓒ **Daily 4.30–11.30 (midnight Fri and Sat)**

🍷🍷 Milestone's ($–$$)

Views across the waterfront promenade and harbor are a fine accompaniment to the food – burgers, steaks, fries, chicken, salads and salmon. Milestone's also does excellent cocktails. In summer there's an outdoor café downstairs on the promenade, where prices are lower.

✉ **812 Wharf Street**
☎ **250/381-2244** Ⓒ **Daily from 11am**

🍷 Pagliacci's ($–$$)

Reservations aren't taken here and it's very popular, so arrive early. The food – a mixture of Italian, Jewish, West Coast and Brooklyn – includes homemade pasta,

chicken and veal, with the restaurant's famous cheesecake taking pride of place on the dessert menu. There's live music most nights.

✉ **1011 Broad Street**
☎ **250/386-1662** Ⓒ **Lunch and dinner daily, plus tea, coffee, drinks and cakes 3–5pm**

Re-Bar ($–$$)

The Re-Bar serves a bewildering variety of juices and other healthy liquid concoctions, as well as an excellent range of mostly organic and vegetarian snacks and meals. It's great for breakfast and lunch, or just to refresh yourself with tea, coffee or a shot of exotic juice.

✉ **50 Bastion Square**
☎ **250/361-9223** Ⓒ **Mon–Thu 8.30am–9pm, Fri–Sat 8.30am–9pm, Sun 8.30am–3.30pm**

Sticky Wicket ($–$$)

The Sticky Wicket is by far the best of Victoria's British-style pubs and is the one most favored by locals. As well as its food and drink, it has a pleasant rooftop patio area and occasional live music.

✉ **Strathcona Hotel, 919 Douglas Street** ☎ **250/383-7137** Ⓒ **Daily**

Swan's Brew Pub ($–$$)

Victoria's nicest and most popular pub-restaurant has ten types of beer on offer from its own brewery, excellent food (including salads, nachos, fish and chips, shepherd's pie), a small hotel and basement nightclub.

✉ **506 Pandora Avenue, corner of Store Street** ☎ **250/361-3310** Ⓒ **Daily 11am–2am**

First Nations Feast

At the Quw'utsun' Cultural and Conference Centre on Vancouver Island, you can enjoy a midday salmon barbecue, with fresh salmon cooked on cedar stakes over an open fire. The food, which includes freshly baked Native Scow Bread and homemade blackberry apple pie, comes on a cedar plank and servers are dressed in traditional costume; there's appropriate entertainment too.

✉ **200 Cowichan Way, Duncan, British Columbia** ☎ **250/746-8119; www.quwutsun.ca**

The Prairies

Taxes
A Goods and Services Tax (GST) of 7 percent is added to all restaurant and café checks. This can be something of a surprise to visitors who are not used to this system, and who are expecting the menu prices to represent the total cost.

Calgary, Alberta
Barley Mill ($)
Stone fireplaces and a 100-year-old Scottish bar create a cozy atmosphere at the Barley Mill, located on the edge of the Eau Claire Market. In summer you can eat and drink outside on the upper-level terrace.
✉ **201 Barclay Parade SW, Eau Claire Market** ☎ **403/290-1500** ◉ **Daily 11am–late**

Earl's ($–$$)
There are seven Earl's locations in Calgary. The menus are long and varied, and often include surprisingly sophisticated dishes from around the world.
✉ **2401 - 4th Street SW** ☎ **403/228-4141** ◉ **Breakfast, lunch and dinner daily**

The James Joyce ($)
The James Joyce is a cut above most mock-Irish bars, with its impressive bar, high ceilings, draft Guinness, carvery lunch and good basic food such as Irish stew, mixed grills and fish and chips. There's usually live Irish music and dancing Wednesday evening and Saturday afternoon and evening.
✉ **114 - 8th Avenue SW** ☎ **403/262-0708** ◉ **Mon–Sat 11am–midnight (also Thu–Sat midnight–1 am), Sun 11.30–11.30**

▼▼▼ River Café ($$–$$$)
More a restaurant than a café, this popular eating place stands in a park by the Bow River, close to the Eau Claire Market. The menu changes regularly and features dishes inspired by the ingredients of the Pacific Northwest (including game). Reservations essential.
✉ **200 - 8th Avenue SE, Prince's Island Park** ☎ **403/261-7670** ◉ **Mon–Fri 11–11, Sat–Sun 10am–11pm (brunch is served on weekends)**

▼▼▼ Teatro ($–$$$)
Teatro is in a grandiose former bank building at the heart of downtown. The inspiration for the food comes from northern Italy, but the cooking also includes Far Eastern and West Coast (fish and seafood) influences.
✉ **200 - 8th Avenue SE** ☎ **403/290-1012** ◉ **Dinner daily, lunch Mon–Fri from 11.30am**

Ship and Anchor ($)
The "Ship" has been Calgary's most popular bar for years. The food and beers are excellent, there's live music some nights, plus sport TV and pub games.
✉ **524 - 17th Avenue SW, corner of 5th Street** ☎ **403/245-3333** ◉ **Daily 11.30am–1.45am**

Edmonton, Alberta
▼▼ The Creperie ($)
Traditional crêpes in a snug French eatery in downtown Edmonton. Vegetarian options plus such dishes as baked salmon and mussels Marseillaise.
www.thecreperie.com ✉ **10220 103rd Street** ☎ **780/420-6656** ◉ **Mon–Fri 11.30–9, Sat 5–10.30, Sun 5–9**

Regina, Saskatchewan
Bushwakker Brewing Co Ltd ($)
A renowned brewpub serving excellent beers and good pub food, such as burgers and fish and chips. There's also a great range of Scotch whiskeys.

www.bushwakker.com ✉ 2206 Dewdney Avenue ☎ 306/359-7276 🕐 Sun–Thu 11am–1am, Fri–Sat 11am–2am

🍷🍷 Mediterranean Bistro ($)
This bistro, just off the TransCanada, has a wide selection of dishes, including such favorites as coq au vin, shrimp seafood ravioli and excellent fish specials, plus some exotic hors d'oeuvres.
✉ 2589 Quance Street E ☎ 306/757-1668 🕐 Daily 11–3, 5–11

Saskatoon, Saskatchewan
Crawdaddy's Louisiana Bar and Grill ($)
As you'd expect, crawfish is on the menu, along with a selection of Creole and Cajun dishes like jambalaya, gumbo and catfish, and there are more traditional choices too.
www.goforthegumbo.com ✉ 244 1st Avenue North ☎ 306/978-2729 🕐 Mon 11–9.30, Tue–Thu 11–10, Fri–Sat 11–midnight, Sun and holidays 4–9.30pm

Winnipeg, Manitoba
Amici ($$)
Sophisticated Italian restaurant serving Tuscan specialties in modern surroundings. Favorite dishes include roast quail, ostrich, wild boar and duck.
www.amiciwpg.com ✉ 326 Broadway ☎ 204/943-4997 🕐 Mon–Fri 11.30–2, 5–11, Sat 5–11

Restaurants in the North
Don't expect every community in the North to have a restaurant. In many places – and this applies particularly in Nunavut – a hotel dining room will be your only option.

The North

Dawson City, Yukon
🍷🍷 Klondike Kate's ($)
Canadian and ethnic-influenced food served in a friendly atmosphere in an old original Gold Rush building. Good vegetarian options. Best known for its breakfasts.
www.klondikekates.ca ✉ 3rd Avenue and King Street ☎ 867/993-6527 🕐 Daily 6.30am–11pm, mid-May to mid-Sep

Whitehorse, Yukon
🍷🍷 Talisman ($)
Great café catering particularly to families and vegetarians. The portions are generous and there's a wide choice of breakfast options.
www.yuk-biz.com/talismancafe ✉ 2112 2nd Avenue ☎ 867/667-2736 🕐 Mon–Wed 9–7, Thu–Sat 9–9, Sun 10–3

Yellowknife, Northwest Territories
L'Atitudes ($)
Good food served throughout the day with a wide choice of dishes from breakfast to dinner.
www.yellowknifeinn.com ✉ Yellowknife Inn, Central Square Mall, 5010 49th Street ☎ 867/873-2601 🕐 Daily 7am–9pm

🍷🍷🍷 L'Heritage Restaurant Francais ($$$)
Elegant French cuisine and a menu heavily influenced by regional ingredients is part of the experience at this gem of a restaurant. There's also an informal bistro downstairs.
✉ 5019 - 49th Street ☎ 867/873-9561 🕐 Tue–Sat 5–10pm

British Columbia & the Rockies

Prices

The prices below are based on the cost of a double room per night.

$ = under $100
$$ = $100–$200
$$$ = $201–$300
$$$$ = over $300

The prices, which were correct at the time of printing, may or may not include the cost of breakfast. Check when you make your reservation.

Diamond Ratings

AAA field inspectors evaluate and rate lodging establishments based on the overall quality and services. AAA's diamond rating criteria reflect the design and service standards set by the lodging industry, combined with the expectations of members.

Properties rated with one (🛇) or two (🛇🛇) diamonds are clean and well-maintained, offering comfortable rooms, with the two diamond property showing enhancements in décor and furnishings. A three (🛇🛇🛇) diamond property shows marked upgrades in physical attributes, services and comfort and may offer additional amenities. A four (🛇🛇🛇🛇) diamond rating signifies a property offering a high level of service and hospitality and a wide variety of amenities and upscale facilities. A five (🛇🛇🛇🛇🛇) diamond rating represents a world-class facility, offering the highest level of luxurious accommodations and personalized guest services.

Banff, Alberta
🛇🛇 Castle Mountain Chalets ($$–$$$)

Between Banff and Lake Louise, at the base of Castle Mountain, this is an excellent base for skiing, hiking and fishing. The one- and two-bedroom log cabins have Jacuzzis, kitchenettes and fireplaces.

www.decorehotels.com ✉ Box 1655, Castle Mountain Junction, on Bow Valley Parkway (Highway 1A) ☎ 403/762-3868

🛇🛇 🛇🛇 Fairmont Banff Springs ($$$$)

This huge Gothic building is one of North America's most famous hotels. It's some way from downtown, but rooms are luxurious and the amenities are excellent – including the superlative spa.

www.fairmont.com/banffsprings ✉ Spray Avenue ☎ 403/762-2211, 1-800-441-1414 (toll free in North America); fax: 403/762-5755

🛇🛇 🛇🛇 Rimrock Resort ($$$–$$$$)

A great place for a bit of pampering, this stunning modern hotel is 2km (1.2 miles) out of town. The spacious, air-conditioned rooms have tasteful furnishings, while the vast main lobby is an architectural splendor.

www.rimrockresort.com ✉ PO Box 1110, 100 Mountain Avenue ☎ 403/762-3356, 1-800-661-1587 (toll free in North America); fax: 403/762-4132

Glacier National Park, British Columbia
🛇🛇🛇 Glacier Park Lodge ($–$$)

This Best Western lodge at the heart of the park also has licensed dining rooms and a 24-hour cafeteria – about the only place to eat in the park.

✉ Glacier National Park, Rogers Pass ☎ 250/837-2126; 1-800-528-1234 (toll free in North America); fax: 250/837-2130

Icefields Parkway, Alberta
🛇🛇🛇 Columbia Icefield Chalet ($$$)

A good place to stop between Banff and Jasper. At least half the rooms have spectacular views of the Athabasca Glacier.

✉ PO Box 1140, Banff; on Icefields Parkway, border of Banff/Jasper national parks ☎ 780/852-6550, 877/423-7433 (toll-free in North America); fax: 780/852-6568 🌑 Closed mid-Oct to mid-May

Jasper, Alberta
🛇🛇🛇 Jasper Park Lodge ($$$$)

Jasper's equivalent of the Fairmont Banff Springs is 5km (3 miles) out of town on Lac Beauvert. It has rustic or modern-style rooms, a golf course, tennis courts, and heated outdoor pool.

www.fairmont.com ✉ PO Box 40, Old Lodge Road ☎ 780/852-3301, 1-800-441-1414 (toll free in North America); fax: 708/852-4946

Kelowna, British Columbia
Lake Okanagan Resort ($$$)

A beautiful lakeside resort about 17km (10.5 miles) from Kelowna, amid 121ha (300 acres) of wooded parkland. Most rooms are on the lakeshore. It has a par-3 golf course, two outdoor pools, tennis courts, marina and beach.

✉ 2751 Westside Road
☎ 250/769-3511, 1-800-663-3273
(toll free in North America);
fax: 250/769-6665

Lake Louise, Alberta

♕♕ ♕♕ Château Lake Louise ($$$)

This famous hotel overlooks beautiful Lake Louise and the Victoria Glacier, and some rooms have private terraces. All meals and activities are included in the rates. The downside is that the area around the hotel frequently gets crowded with day visitors.

www.fairmont.com ✉ Lake Louise Drive ☎ 403/522-3511; fax: 403/522-3834

♕♕ ♕♕ Lake Louise Inn ($–$$)

This is the most reasonably priced place to stay in the entire Lake Louise area (aside from the youth hostel), and offers a variety of rooms in a spacious five-building complex. The rooms are very comfortable and guest amenities include an indoor swimming pool.

www.lakelouiseinn.com ✉ 210 Village Road, Lake Louise Village ☎ 403/522-3791, 1-800-661-9237 (toll free in North America); fax: 403/522-2018

Vancouver, British Columbia

♕♕ ♕♕ The Fairmont Waterfront ($$$–$$$$)

An elegant and luxurious 23-story hotel in the spectacular Canada Place complex on Vancouver's harbor. Most rooms have superb views over Burrard Inlet to the mountains, and all contain original modern Canadian art. It has a health club and outdoor pool.

www.fairmont.com ✉ 900 Canada Place Way ☎ 604/691-1991, 1-800-441-1414 (toll free in North America); fax: 604/691-1828

♕♕ ♕♕ Four Seasons ($$$$)

The Four Seasons is at the heart of the shopping and financial districts. Rooms are fairly small, but deluxe rooms and suites are available. The interior is luxurious, and the health club, pool and fitness center are first class.

✉ 791 West Georgia Street ☎ 604/689-9333, 1-800-268-6282 (toll free in Canada), 1-800-332-3442 (toll free in North America); fax: 604/684-4555

♕♕ Sandman Hotel ($$)

The Sandman is a good mid-price chain, with hotels across western Canada. The Vancouver hotel is within walking distance of Gastown and the central sights. Rooms are comfortable, and amenities include a sauna and indoor swimming pool.

www.sandmanhotels.com ✉ 180 West Georgia Street ☎ 604/681-2211, 1-800-SANDMAN (toll free in North America); fax: 604/681-8009

Whistler, British Columbia

♕♕ ♕ Durlacher Hof Alpine Inn ($$–$$$)

An authentic-looking alpine chalet run by an Austrian family. Rooms and suites are all tastefully decorated, and those on the top floor have vaulted, pine-clad ceilings.

www.durlacherhof.com ✉ 7055 Nestors Road ☎ 604/932-1924; fax 604/938-1980

♕♕ ♕♕ Westin Resort and Spa ($$$$)

Spectacular mountain views, excellent leisure amenities and superb cuisine are on offer here. The suites have modern furnishings and the spa is one of Canada's finest.

www.westinwhistler.com ✉ 4090 Whistler Way ☎ 604/905-5000; fax: 604/905-5640

Bed-and-Breakfast

Bed-and-breakfast or guest-house accommodations are available in most towns and cities. Tourist offices generally have detailed listings. Rooms do not always have private bathrooms and breakfasts range from "continental" – usually a bread roll or muffin and coffee – to a full hot breakfast. Check the location, as some places can be some way out of town and city centers. For more information contact the Western Canada Bed & Breakfast Innkeepers Association (☎ 604/255-9199) or the BC Bed & Breakfast Association (☎ 604/734-3486).

The Pacific Coast

Reservations

It is important to make reservations during peak seasons, usually July and August, and when there are special events, such as the Calgary Stampede. At other times you should call a few days in advance to secure a room. Make sure you cancel in good time or you may be charged a night's fee. Confirm check-in times – rooms in some hotels may not be available until mid- or late afternoon.

Nanaimo, British Columbia

⬡⬡⬡ Best Western Dorchester Hotel ($$$)

A boutique-style hotel with elegant guest rooms overlooking the harbor and city. The service is excellent and the central location a definite plus.

www.dorchesternanaimo.com
✉ 70 Church Street ☎ 250/754-6835; fax: 250/754-2638

Tofino, British Columbia

⬡⬡ ⬡⬡ Wickaninnish Inn ($$$)

Spectacularly set on a rocky headland on Vancouver Island's rugged west coast, close to the Pacific Rim National Park, this inn has 75 rooms with magnificent ocean and beach views, and private balconies to take full advantage of them. Other features include fireplaces, down comforters and oversize soaker tubs.

www.wickinn.com
✉ Osprey Lane at Chesterman Beach, PO Box 250, Tofino ☎ 250/725-3100, 800/333-4606; fax: 250/725-3110

Victoria, British Columbia

⬡⬡⬡ Abigail's ($$$)

Located only three blocks from the Inner Harbour and all the attractions of downtown Victoria, this is a lovely small hotel. The 23 rooms are all beautifully furnished with antiques, and some have Jacuzzis and fireplaces. A gourmet breakfast is included in the price

www.abigailshotel.com
✉ 906 McClure Street ☎ 250/388-5363, 800/561-6565; fax: 250/388-7787

⬡⬡⬡ Best Western Carlton Plaza ($–$$)

The Carlton Plaza's modern, air-conditioned rooms provide a comfortable base close to downtown's main sights and shopping areas. Suites are available, and there are units with kitchens.

www.bestwesterncarltonplaza.com ✉ 642 Johnson Street ☎ 250/388-5513, 1-800-663-7241 (toll free in North America); fax: 250/388-5343

⬡⬡⬡ ⬡⬡⬡ Fairmont Empress Hotel ($$–$$$$)

The Empress is a Victoria icon and an imposing sight in its central position close to the Parliament Building and overlooking the Inner Harbour. Having some 460 rooms, it is a big and busy hotel. Service is excellent, as are the amenities, and all the rooms are well-furnished. Elegant afternoon teas, in true British style, are served to some 80,000 visitors a year (➤ 96, panel)

www.fairmont.com
✉ 721 Government Street, V8W 1W5 ☎ 250/384-8111, 1-800-441-1414 (toll free in North America); fax: 250/381-4334

⬡⬡ ⬡⬡ James Bay Inn ($–$$)

One of the oldest hotels in Victoria, in operation since 1911, this is a good low-cost option with a central location and quite a history – it was home to the renowned British Columbia painter Emily Carr for a while just before her death. Also on the premises is the Colonial Café and JBI pub.

www.jamesbayinn.bc.ca
✉ 270 Government Street ☎ 250/384-7151, 800/836-2649; fax: 250/385-2311

The Prairies

Calgary, Alberta
🍷🍷🍷 Fairmont Palliser ($$$)

The Palliser is Calgary's most prestigious hotel. All the rooms are spacious, air-conditioned and decorated in traditional style, and there is a steam room, health club and exercise equipment on site.

✉ 113 9th Avenue SW
☎ 403/262-1234, 1-800-441-1414 (toll free in North America); fax: 403/260-1260

🍷🍷🍷 Sandman Hotel Downtown Calgary ($$)

The rooms here have excellent views, and are spacious and comfortable. Amenities include an indoor swimming pool and fitness center, and there is a Dennys' Restaurant adjacent (open 24 hours).

www.sandman.ca ✉ 888-7th Avenue SW ☎ 403/237-8626, 1-800-726-3626(toll free in North America); fax: 403/290-1238

Drumheller, Alberta
🍷🍷🍷 Inn at Heartwood Manor ($$–$$$)

All the rooms are individually designed in this delightful old clapboard heritage building. The spa facilities are superb – ideal for those in need of some pampering.

www.innsatheartwood.com
✉ 320 North Railway Avenue E
☎ 403/823-6495; fax: 403/823-4935

Edmonton, Alberta
🍷🍷🍷 Union Bank Inn ($$$–$$$$)

A luxury hotel in the heart of downtown, offering the ultimate in comfort and elegance. The rooms are decorated in pastel shades and some bathrroms have jet tubs.

www.unionbankinn.com
✉ 10053 Jasper Avenue
☎ 780/423-3600, 888/423-3601 (toll free in Canada); fax: 780/423-4623

The North

Accommodations in the north can be hard to find, although in the larger cities, such as Dawson City, Whitehorse and Yellowknife, there is usually a good choice. Farther afield you will find some of the smaller settlements may have only one option, and prices are not particularly low – be prepared to pay around $100 or more for a room per night. Camping is always an option, if you come prepared.

The North

Dawson City, Yukon
🍷🍷 Eldorado Hotel ($–$$)

In the heart of Dawson City. Rooms are bright and comfortable and there are executive suites and apartments with kitchens.

www.eldoradohotel.ca
✉ Corner of 3rd and Princess Street ☎ 867/993-5451; fax: 867/993-5256

🍷🍷 Westmark Inn ($–$$)

The renovated Westmark is a spacious, comfortable complex renowned for its Klondike barbecues. Some of the modern rooms and suites have kitchens and the dining room is open throughout the day.

www.westmarkhotels.com
✉ 5th and Harper streets
☎ 867/993-5542; fax: 867/993-5623

Whitehorse, NWT
🍷🍷🍷 Hawkins House ($$)

Bright and airy Victorian-style bed-and-breakfast with polished hardwood floors and soft yellow walls. Some rooms have a whirlpool tub.

✉ 303 Hawkins Street
☎ 867/668-7638; fax: 867/669-7632

British Columbia & the Rockies

Sales Tax

Canada has a Goods and Services Tax (GST) of 7 percent on most good and services, plus Provincial Sales Tax (PST), which varies from province to province – oil-rich Alberta has none at all.

Tax Refunds

The Government Sales Tax (GST) that is added to hotel bills and certain goods purchased can be reclaimed by non-residents on leaving the country. Claim forms are available from airports, many stores and hotels. All receipts (originals, not photocopies) must be enclosed with the forms. For further information contact the Canadian Embassy in your home country.

Arts & Crafts

Crafthouse

An imaginative range of ceramics, fabrics, furniture and glass, along with metal and wood objects.
www.cabc.net ✉ 1386 Cartwright Street, Granville Island, Vancouver, British Columbia ☎ 604/687-7270 ⏰ Daily 10.30–5.30. Closed Mon in Jan

Books & Music

Banff Book and Art Den

A vast selection of maps and guidebooks.
www.banffbooks.com ✉ 94 Banff Avenue, ✉ Banff, Alberta ☎ 403/762-3919

Blackberry Books

It's a pleasure browsing around this tiny store, with its good selection of novels, travel guides, general titles and specialist subjects, including art, architecture and cooking.
www.bbooks.ca ✉ 1663 Duranleau Street, Granville Island, Vancouver, British Columbia ☎ 604/685-4113 ⏰ Daily 9–6

Chapters

This nationwide chain is the best place to come for books, maps and travel guides. Open to 11pm daily.
✉ 788 Robson Street, corner of Howe Street, Vancouver, British Columbia ☎ 604/682-4066

Virgin Megastore

Canada's largest music store, housed in Vancouver's former public library. Great selection of videos, books and computer games.
✉ 788 Burrard Street, corner of Robson Street, Vancouver, British Columbia ☎ 604/669-2289 ⏰ Daily 10–10

Clothes & Accessories

Brick Shirt House

Great outdoor clothing. The hats, T-shirts and sweaters make great souvenirs.
✉ C-4227 Village Stroll, Whistler, British Columbia ☎ 604/932-5320 ⏰ Daily 8am–11pm

Intra-Venus

Footwear that's both trendy and comfortable, plus casual clothing and accessories.
www.intra-venus.com ✉ 1072 Mainland Street, Yaletown, Vancouver, British Columbia ☎ 604/685-9696 ⏰ Mon–Wed and Sat 11–7, Thu–Fri 11–8, Sun noon–5 (reduced hours in winter)

Leone

Fashion store selling such labels as Armani, Dolce and Gabbana, Hugo Boss and Versace. Valet parking.
www.leone.ca ✉ 757 West Hastings Street, Sinclair Centre, Vancouver, British Columbia ☎ 604/683-1133 ⏰ Mon–Fri 9.30–6, Sat 9.30–5.30, Sun noon–5

First Nations Art

Banff Indian Trading Post

Superb selection of Amerindian goods – arts, crafts, jewelry, clothing etc.
✉ Cave Avenue, corner of Birch Avenue, Banff, Alberta ☎ 403/762-2456

Dorothy Grant

Beautiful First Nations clothes and artifacts in traditional Haida designs. The store even resembles a Haida longhouse.
✉ Sinclair Centre, 250–757 West Hastings Street, Vancouver, British Columbia ☎ 604/681-0201

Images for a Canadian Heritage

High quality contemporary and traditional aboriginal art at one of Canada's finest galleries.

www.imagesforcanada.com
164 Water Street, Gastown, Vancouver, British Columbia
604/685-7046, 877/212-8900

Inuit Gallery of Vancouver

Works by Inuit and First Nations artists – soapstone animal sculptures, traditional masks, jewelry, gift items and boxes.

www.inuit.com **206 Cambie Street, Gastown, Vancouver, British Columbia 604/688-7323, 888/615-8399**

Food & Drink
Summerhill Estate Winery

One of the best wineries in the Okanagan area. Tours are followed by a chance to sample and buy the wine.

www.summerhill.bc.ca **4870 Chute Lake Road, Kelowna, British Columbia 250/764-8000, 800/667-3538 (toll free in North America)**

Household Good & Interior Design
Chintz & Company

Fabrics, furnishings, accessories and gifts, as well as many smaller items such as candles, lamps and assorted *objets d'art*.

www.chintz.com **950 Homer Street, Vancouver, British Columbia 604/689-2022**
Mon–Sat 10–6, Sun 11–5

Malls & Department Stores
The Bay

Part of a chain throughout Canada. It's come a long way from the original Hudson's Bay Company trading posts, but is still owned by the historic company. The merchandise is varied and high quality.
674 Granville Street, Vancouver, BC 604/681-3211

The Landing

A classy mall, built around a restored 1915 heritage warehouse in Gastown.
375 Water Street, Vancouver, British Columbia 604/482-6007

Metrotown

Around 500 stores, more than 20 movie theaters and the Entertainment Centre make this the second-largest shopping mall in the world (the largest is in Edmonton, ▶ 77 and 108).
www.metrotown.info **4800 Kingsway, Burnaby, Vancouver, British Columbia 604/438-4700, 604/630-3340**

Pacific Centre

With more than 200 stores, this is one of Vancouver's best malls, in a great downtown location.
www.pacificcentre.com **700 West Georgia Street, Vancouver, British Columbia 604/688-7235**

Sinclair Centre

Four historic buildings – the Post Office, Federal Building, Customs Warehouse and Winch Building – have been converted into this sophisticated mall.
www.sinclaircentre.com
757 West Hastings Street, Vancouver, British Columbia 604/659-1009

Markets
Granville Island Public Market

One of North America's finest food markets with a stunning array of meat, fish, cheese, fruit, wine and specialist food stands. You can get just about anything you're looking for – from fruit and vegetables to fresh local oysters and salmon.
www.granvilleisland.com
Johnston Street, Granville Island, Vancouver, British Columbia 604/666-6655, 604/666-5784

Robson Street

Vancouver's main shopping street, filled with trendy boutiques, upscale stores, sidewalk cafés and restaurants, is also the focus of much of the city's colorful streetlife in summer. It was once described by the late fashion designer, Gianni Versace, as "one of the ten streets in the world where you have to have a store."

Opening Hours

Most stores open Monday to Saturday, from 10 to 6, often with late opening Thursday and Friday evenings. Shopping malls usually have longer hours, from 7.30am to 9pm. Sunday opening times are being relaxed and stores are generally open from noon to 5pm. Most towns have at least one pharmacy that is open 24 hours a day (usually on a rotating system).

Lonsdale Quay Market

At the Seabus terminal, this is a great place to shop or simply soak up its sights, smells and sounds. Lots of food counters and outdoor eating areas, plus fantastic views and entertainment every day.

✉ **Lonsdale Quay, 123 Carrie Cates Court, North Vancouver, British Columbia** ☎ **604/985-6261**

Specialty Stores

Canadian Impressions

One of Vancouver's better souvenir shops; great for typical Canadian goods like maple syrup, salmon jerky and lumberjack shirts. (Also on Burrard and Water streets.)

✉ **601 Cordova Street, Vancouver, British Columbia** ☎ **604/681-3507**

The Fudgery

The smell of fudge and chocolate will tempt you inside, where you can watch the sweetmeats being made by hand before you buy them.

www.thefudgery.com ✉ **215 Banff Avenue, Banff, Alberta** ☎ **403/762-3003**

Murchie's Tea & Coffee

Murchie's has been selling fine tea and coffee for more than a century, but now in this new location. You can also buy coffeemakers and teapots and get afternoon tea (▶ 96, panel).

✉ **825 West Pender Street. Also at 1200 Homer Street, Vancouver, British Columbia** ☎ **604/669-0783**

Okanagan Opal

Canada's only opal mine has a store selling attractive jewelry designed in its own studio. Stones in many different shades are incorporated into necklaces, bracelets, rings and more. In summer you can dig for opals (Fri–Sun).

www.opalscanada.com ✉ **7879 Highway 97, Vernon, British Columbia; 6.4km (4 miles) north of Vernon; take Pleasant Valley exit and follow signs** ☎ **250/542-1103**

Salmagundi West

Specializing in a wide range of antiques and collectibles, this place is worth a visit just to see the fascinating things they've got in store.

✉ **321 West Cordova Street, Gastown, Vancouver, British Columbia** ☎ **604/681-4648**

The Source

A great place for all sorts of unusual gifts, with an emphasis on British pub memorabilia.

www.sourceenterprises.bc.ca ✉ **929 Main Street, Vancouver, British Columbia** ☎ **604/684-9914**

Spirit of the North

Canada's largest tax- and duty-free store – now you don't have to shop at the airport.

✉ **1026 Alberni Street, Vancouver, British Columbia** ☎ **604/683-2416**

Totem Ski Shop

Great outdoors wear, including a fine range of footwear, sweatshirts and handknit Cowichan sweaters, which make great souvenirs.

www.totemskishop.com or www.jasper.ca/totems ✉ **408 Connaught Drive, Jasper, Alberta** ☎ **780/852-3078**

The Pacific Coast

Art & Antiques
Antique Row
Home to over two dozen antiques shops, this is a great place for browsing.
✉ **Fort Street, between Blanshard and Cook, Victoria, British Columbia**

Books
Book Store on Bastion Street
In addition to its big range of reading matter, there are storytelling sessions and book readings. Located in a fine historic building.
✉ **76 Bastion Street, Nanaimo, British Columbia** ☎ **250/753-2023**

Clothing
Jan Donaldson Designs
The home and studio of the fiber artist and clothing designer who hosted her own TV crafts show when she lived in Montréal. Make an appointment, or just call in and hope she's at home.
✉ **3237 Ash Road, Chemainus, British Columbia** ☎ **250/246-2348, 1-800/442-6446**

First Nations Art & Crafts
Cowichan Trading Co. Ltd.
First Nations crafts and a wide range of souvenirs, including jewelry and moccasins.
✉ **1328 Government Street, Victoria, British Columbia** ☎ **250/383-0321**

Hill's Native Art
This was the first Hill's store to open (in 1946) to provide an outlet for First Nations artists. Now it's one of five (others are in Nanaimo, Victoria and Vancouver), and stocks a wide range of art, crafts and clothing.

www.royalmuseumshop.com
✉ **Koksilah, 1.6km (1 mile) south of Duncan, British Columbia** ☎ **250/746-6731**

Royal British Columbia Museum Shop
First Nations artwork including gold and silver jewelry, ceremonial sticks, totem poles and masks. You don't have to pay museum admission to visit the shop.
www.royalmuseumshop.com
✉ **675 Belleville Street, Victoria, British Columbia** ☎ **250/356-0505**

Food & Drink
Roger's Chocolates
The place to shop for sublime hand-crafted, preservative-free chocolates.
✉ **913 Government Street, Victoria, British Columbia** ☎ **250/727-6851**

Malls & Department Stores
The Bay
Victoria's key department store, with a huge and varied selection of goods.
✉ **1150 Douglas Street, British Columbia** ☎ **250/385-1311**

Market Square
One of Victoria's main shopping areas with three levels of stores.
✉ **560 Johnson Street, Victoria, British Columbia** ☎ **250/386-2441**

Market
Salt Spring Island Saturday Market
This Gulf island is renowned for its artist/artisan community and for its organic market gardens. Their combined output is on sale here.
✉ **Centennial Park, Ganges**

Fan Tan Alley
One of the best little streets in Victoria's Chinatown is Fan Tan Alley. The narrowest street in the country, in places it is only the width of an armspan. It used to be filled with brothels, opium dens and gambling joints, but these days it is lined with tiny stores selling a variety of goods, from New Age crystals to bric-à-brac.

The Prairies

Winter Warmth
Because of its ferocious winters, most of Calgary's shops are undercover in malls and shopping centers. The main malls downtown are located between 5th Street SW and 1st Street SE, along 8th Avenue. For a list of stores get a copy of the free monthly *Where Calgary* magazine, available from hotels and the visitor center.

Antiques
Antique Exchange and Warehouse
Two warehouses stocking antique furniture and lots more. Great for browsing.
⊠ 370 Donald and 41 Princess Street, Winnipeg, Manitoba
☎ 204/943-1315

Emporium Antique Mall
Western Canada's largest antiques mall, in a historic 1911 building.
⊠ Saskatoon Emporium, 126 20th Street West, Saskatoon, Saskatchewan ☎ 306/653-5595

Books
Book and Brier Patch
A large independent store with more than 30,000 titles on offer.
⊠ 4065 Albert Street, Regina, Saskatchewan ☎ 306/586-5814

Clothes & Accessories
Alberta Boot
Thousands of boots and shoes made from cow hide, alligator, kangaroo and snake. It's pricey, but the quality is excellent. Also jeans, hats, shirts and belts.
www.albertaboot.com ⊠ 614 10th Avenue SW, Calgary, Alberta ☎ 403/263-4605

Smithbilt Hats
The place to buy a Stetson for the Stampede. They also make great souvenirs.
⊠ 1235 10th Avenue SW, Calgary, Alberta ☎ 403/244-9131

Winnipeg Outfitters
Western wear and First Nations handicrafts. Cold-weather gear a specialty.
250 McPhillips Street, Winnipeg, Manitoba
☎ 204/775-9653

Crafts & Jewelry
Manitoba Museum of Man and Nature Shop
Local arts and crafts highlighting the province's history and cultural heritage.
⊠ 190 Rupert Avenue, Winnipeg, Manitoba
☎ 204/988-0615

First Nations Art
Bayat Gallery
Inuit artists from Canada's Arctic showcase their work here.
www.inuitgallery.com ⊠ 163 Stafford Street, Winnipeg, Manitoba ☎ 204/475-5873

Northern Images
Highlights the work of Inuit and Déné artists.
⊠ 393 Portage Avenue, Winnipeg, Manitoba
☎ 204/942-5501

Malls & Shopping Complexes
West Edmonton Mall
The world's biggest shopping mall, with more than 800 stores (▶ 77).
www.westedmall.com ⊠ 8882 170th Street, Edmonton, Alberta
☎ 403/444-5200

Markets
Eau Claire Festival Market
A vibrant mix of food stands, specialty stores, bars, cafés and restaurants.
www.eauclairemarket.com ⊠ 200 Barclay Parade Southwest, Calgary, Alberta
☎ 403/264-6450

The Forks Market
Winnipeg's best shopping experience, with specialty foods, fresh produce and arts and crafts.
www.theforks.com ⊠ 201 One Forks Market Road, Winnipeg, Manitoba ☎ 204/942-6302

The North

Arts & Crafts
Midnight Sun Gallery and Gifts
A wealth of local arts and crafts, including jewelry, posters and pottery.
www.midnightsunyukon.com
✉ 205C Main Street, Whitehorse, Yukon ☎ 867/668-4350

Books
Mac's Fireweed Books
One of the Yukon's best-known bookstores, stocking a great selection of books about the Yukon, pioneer days and the Klondike Gold Rush; also bestsellers, magazines and newspapers.
www.yukonbooks.com ✉ 203 Main Street, Whitehorse, Yukon ☎ 867/668-6104, 800/661-0508

The Yellowknife Book Cellar
As well as the usual current titles, the Yellowknife Book Cellar has a good line in books on northern and native studies.
✉ 48th Street (in Panda II Mall) Yellowknife, NWT ☎ 867/920-2220

Clothes & Accessories
Folknits
Specializes in unusual fibers such as qiviut (the down of the musk ox and one of the rarest natural fibers in the world); also has clothes made from arctic fox fur, mountain goat wool and regular yarns.
www.folknits.yukon.net
✉ 2151 2nd Avenue, Whitehorse, Yukon ☎ 867/668-7771

Unique Tailors
A good choice of outdoor wear – parkas, jackets, hats and gloves, as well as great First Nations clothing and accessories.
www.uniquetailors-yukon.com
✉ 4101 4th Avenue, Whitehorse, Yukon ☎ 867/633-6088

Wolverine Sports Shop
Downtown store selling an excellent range of outdoor wear and camping gear.
✉ Stantons Plaza, 100 Borden Drive, Yellowknife, NWT ☎ 867/873-4350

Jewelry
Goldsmiths
Original jewelry and metal art designed and created in the store. You can also buy Yukon gold nuggets here.
www.yukoninfo.com/goldsmith
✉ 106 Main Street, Whitehorse, Yukon ☎ 867/667-7340

Markets
Bonanza Market
Fresh fruit and vegetables, and a good delicatessen. Great for browsing and meeting the locals.
✉ 2nd Avenue and Princess Street, Bag 5020, Dawson City, Yukon ☎ 867/993-6567

Specialty Stores
Klondike Nugget and Ivory Shop
Exquisite jewelry is made here using Dawson gold nuggets – in business for more than 90 years.
✉ Front and Queen streets, Dawson City, Yukon ☎ 867/993-5432

Tgit Geomatics Ltd
Aeronautical and hydrographic charts, plus a good selection of maps of the north.
✉ 101 - 5016 Franklin Avenue, Yellowknife, NWT ☎ 867/873-8448

First Nations Art
The Inuit have a long tradition of using materials around them such as soapstone, baleen, ivory, bone, antler, skin and wood to create intricate and elaborately carved everyday objects like combs, pins and snow goggles. Almost every community in the Arctic has its own cooperative that helps locals artists and artisans to market and sell their wares. For a complete list, contact Nunavut Tourism, PO Box 1450, Iqaluit, Nunavut, tel: 800/491-7910.

Where to take the Children

Sleepovers

All kids love a sleepover and these are now possible at a number of attractions. The best must surely be the opportunity to roll out your sleeping bag beside the beluga whale tank at Vancouver Aquarium, and drift off to sleep while these magnificent creatures swim around beside you. In addition, kids (who must be accompanied by an adult) get a special tour after closing time, various activities, a light supper and breakfast. Sleepovers are on specific nights; call the Aquarium on 604/659-3504 for information (► 34).

British Columbia & the Rockies

Britannia Beach, British Columbia

BC Museum of Mining

Climb aboard the train for an underground tour of the old mines (► 18).

www.bcmuseumofmining.org
✉ Highway 99; 51.5km (32 miles) north of Vancouver on Sea-to-Sky Highway
☎ 604/896-2233, 800/896-4044
🕐 Daily 9–4.30, early May to mid-Oct; Mon–Fri 9–4.30, rest of year

Vancouver, British Columbia

Alcan Children's Maritime Discovery Centre

Educational fun for toddlers and younger kids.

www.vmm.bc.ca ✉ Vancouver Maritime Museum, 1095 Ogden Avenue ☎ 604/257-8300
🕐 Daily 10–5. Closed Mon in winter 🚢 Aquabus

H. R. MacMillan Space Centre

Space-related activities, including a realistic virtual voyage in a spacecraft simulator, multimedia show and planetarium.

www.hrmacmillanspacecentre.com ✉ 1100 Chestnut Street
☎ 604/738-7827 🕐 Daily 10–5. Closed Mon in off season
🚢 Aquabus

Vancouver Aquarium
► 34

Whistler, British Columbia

Adventure Zone

Activities include zooming down Blackcomb Mountain on a luge, mini-golf, horseback riding and a climbing wall.

www.mywhistler.com
✉ Whistler ☎ 604/938-2769, 877/991-9988 🕐 Daily 10–6 late Jun–early Sep (also 6–8 Sat) depending on weather

The Pacific Coast

Victoria, British Columbia

Victoria Bug Zoo

Children will be in their element among some of the most incredible looking insects and other creepy-crawlies – they even get to hold some of them.

www.bugzoo.bc.ca ✉ 631 Courtney Street ☎ 250/384-2847
🕐 Daily 9–9, Jun–Labour Day weekend; Mon–Sat 9.30–5.30, Sun 11–5.30, rest of year

The Prairies

Calgary, Alberta

Butterfield Acres

A hands-on farm where children can take part in daily chores, from milking to collecting eggs.

www.butterfieldacres.com
✉ 254077 Rocky Ridge Road; 3.2km (2 miles) north of the Crowchild Trail – Highway 1A
☎ 403/547-3595 🕐 Daily 10–4, Jul–Aug; Mon–Fri 10–2, Sat–Sun 10–4, Apr–Jun and Sep; winter special events by advance ticket purchase only

Calaway Park

Thrills and spills for children of all ages at western Canada's largest outdoor amusement park, with rides, mini-golf, a haunted mansion and more.

www.calawaypark.com
✉ 254033 Range Road 33; 10km (6 miles) west of Calgary on TransCanada Highway at Springbank Road ☎ 403/240-3822 🕐 Daily 10–8, late

Jun–Aug; Fri 5–10, Sat–Sun 10–8, mid-May to mid-Jun; Sat–Sun 11–6, Sep to mid-Oct

Calgary Zoo, Botanical Gardens and Prehistoric Park ► 68

Edmonton, Alberta
The Odyssium
Fun for all the family, with galleries including Mystery Avenue, DiscoveryLand, Space Place and Gallery of the Gross. Also observatory and IMAX theater.

www.odyssium.com ✉ 11211 – 142 Street ☎ 780/452-9100 🕒 Sun–Thu 10–5, Fri–Sat 10–9. IMAX theater: from 11am

West Edmonton Mall
The world's largest indoor amusement park, and a great way to get the children excited about visiting a shopping center ► 77.

Regina, Saskatchewan
Maxwell's Amusements
Karts, bumper boats and the Waterpark are the main attractions, along with mini-golf and batting cages.

www.maxwellsamusements. com ✉ Victoria Avenue E ☎ 306/789-6200 🕒 Daily 11–10, Jun–Aug; reduced hours early Apr–May and Sep–early Oct, depending on weather

Winnipeg, Manitoba
Fort Whyte Centre
Your children will learn a great deal about nature while they are having fun here. There are more than 160ha (400 acres) of woods, lakes and grassland, which are home to a herd of bison, a prairie dog town and an aquarium.

www.fortwhyte.org ✉ 1961 McCreary Road ☎ 204/989-8355 🕒 Mon–Fri 9–5, Sat–Sun 10–5 (extended hours Jun–Oct)

Manitoba Children's Museum ► 64

Manitoba Theatre for Young People
Performances for young people are staged here by a professional theater company, as well as classes in acting, animation, broadcasting and filmmaking.

www.mtyp.ca ✉ CanWest Global Performing Arts Centre, Forks Market Road, The Forks ☎ 204/942-8898, 877/871-6897 (toll free in Canada) 🕒 Fri 7pm, Sat–Sun 1pm and 4pm, Oct–May 💲 $10–12 🚌 Free shuttle

The North

Dawson City, Yukon
GoldBottom Mine Tours
Finding a glittering fragment of gold among the gravel evokes the excitement of the Gold Rush. You get a tour with guides who tell lots of fascinating stories before they let you loose on the creek. You keep what you pan, and you might even see bear or moose. Wear sturdy footwear.

www.goldbottom.com ✉ Hunker Creek Road; east of Dawson City, 14.5km (9 miles) south of intersection of Klondike Highway North and Hunker Creek Road ☎ 867/993-5023 🕒 Daily 11–7, Jun until freeze-up

Whitehorse, Yukon
Beringia
This splendid interpretive center presents the Yukon as it was when wooly mammoths roamed the area 40,000 years ago, and it's mammoth skeleton is a major attraction for children. They will also also be thrilled by the scimitar cats and the unbelievably huge giant beavers.

www.beringia.com ✉ Mile 915 (Km1,473) Alaska Highway, next to Whitehorse International Airport ✉ 867/667-8855 🕒 Daily 8.30–7, Jun–Aug; 9–6, mid-May to Jun, Sep; Sun 1–5 or by appointment rest of year

Dogsled trips
Kids and dogs go well together, and one of the great experiences you can offer your children in the North is to explore it in the time-honored way – by dogsled. And though nothing beats taking this trip in the snow, you don't *have* to brave the winter cold – Blue Kennels run trips at any time of year, and in summer the dogs pull buggies instead of sleds.

www.bluekennels.de ✉ Box 31523; 50km (31 miles) west of Whitehorse at Mile 950 on the Alaska Highway ☎ 867/633-2219 🕒 Call for details

Theatres & Performance

Theatre Under the Stars

Open-air performances may lack the atmosphere of a theater, but there is something quite special about being out in the fresh air on a balmy summer evening and watching a top-class performance as the stars (the ones in the sky, that is) begin to twinkle. The Theatre Under the Stars is a non-profit company that stages popular musicals at the Malkin Bowl in Vancouver's Stanley Park.
☎ 604/687-0174 ◉ Mid-Jul to late Aug

British Columbia & the Rockies

Banff, Alberta
The Banff Centre
Arts, culture and conference venue with a varied program of events.
www.banffcentre.ca ✉ 107 Tunnel Mountain Drive (on slope of Tunnel Mountain, four blocks east from Banff Avenue)
☎ 403/762-6100 (or 6301 for box office) ◉ Year-round

Chemainus, British Columbia
Chemainus Theatre
An intimate dinner theater with a good selection of new and classic musicals and drama.
www.chemainustheatrefestival.ca ✉ 9737 Chemainus Road
☎ 250/246-9820 or 800/565-7738 ◉ Year-round

Vancouver, British Columbia
Bard on the Beach
Picnic in the park and watch a Shakespeare play.
www.bardonthebeach.org ✉ Theatre Tent, Vanier Park
☎ 604/739 0559, 877/739-0559 ◉ Tue–Sun, mid-Jun to late Sep

Firehall Arts Centre
A variety of events, including dance, music, theater and comedy.
www.firehallartscentre.ca ✉ 280 East Cordova Street
☎ 604/689-0926 ◉ Year-round

Orpheum
This opulent 1927 theater reopened in 1977 as the permanent home of the Vancouver Symphony.
www.city.vancouver.bc.ca/theatres/orpheum/orpheum.html ✉ 884 Granville Street
☎ 604/665-3050 ◉ Year-round

Queen Elizabeth Theatre Complex
Comprises the Vancouver Playhouse and the Queen Elizabeth Theatre, home of the Vancouver Opera and Ballet. Mostly classical.
✉ 600 Hamilton Street
☎ 604/665-3050 ◉ Year-round

Whistler, British Columbia
Rainbow Theatre
The best movie theater in Whistler, playing a new feature each week. It also hosts the Whistler Film Festival.
www.mywhistler.com ✉ 4010 Whistler Way ☎ 604/932-2422

The Pacific Coast

Victoria, British Columbia
Belfry
This old church is now a theater, producing high-quality shows; also hosts pop and jazz concerts.
www.belfry.bc.ca ✉ 1291 Gladstone Avenue ☎ 250/385-6815 ◉ Aug to mid-May

Langham Court
A former carriage house and barn has been converted into this fully functional theater, staging classical and new drama and comedies.
www.langhamcourttheatre.bc.ca ✉ 805 Langham Court
☎ 250/384-2142 ◉ Year-round

Royal and McPherson
The Victoria Symphony and the Pacific Opera Victoria are based in this superb early 20th-century building with a full calendar of shows.
www.rmts.bc.ca ✉ 805 Broughton Street ☎ 250/386-6121, 888/717-6121 ◉ Year-round

The Prairies

Calgary, Alberta
EPCOR Centre for the Performing Arts
A six-level complex offering drama, dance and comedy.
www.theartscentre.org
✉ 205 8th Avenue Southeast
☎ 403/294-7455 ◷ Year-round

Southern Alberta Jubilee Auditorium
Home to the Calgary Opera and Alberta Ballet. Classical music, opera, drama and rock and pop concerts.
www.jubileeauditorium.com/southern ✉ 1415 14th Avenue Northwest ☎ 403/297-8000 ◷ Year-round

Edmonton, Alberta
Citadel Theatre
One of Canada's top live performing arts complexes.
www.citadeltheatre.com
✉ 9828 – 101A Avenue ☎ 780/425-1820, 888/425-1820 (toll free in Canada) ◷ Year-round

Francis Winspear Centre for Music
The Edmonton Symphony is based at this world-class hall, which hosts various events.
www.winspearcentre.com
✉ Sir Winston Churchill Square
☎ 780/428-1414, 800/563-5081 ◷ Year-round

Regina, Saskatchewan
Globe Theatre
Theater in the round by Saskatchewan's oldest professional company.
www.globetheatrelive.com
✉ 1801 Scarth Street
☎ 306/525-6400 ◷ Year-round

Saskatchewan Centre of the Arts
This complex is home to Opera Saskatchewan.
www.centreofthearts.sk.ca
✉ 200 Lakeshore Drive
☎ 306/525-9999, 800/667-8497 (toll free in North America) ◷ Year-round

Winnipeg, Manitoba
Burton Cummings Theatre
Renamed after the local rock star (of The Guess Who), who has given financial support to save this fine heritage theater.
✉ 364 Smith Street ☎ 204/956-5656 ◷ Year-round

Centennial Concert Hall
Manitoba's premier performance facility with a full and varied program.
www.mbccc.ca ✉ 555 Main Street ☎ 204/957-1360 ◷ Year-round

Manitoba Theatre Centre
World-class performances in Canada's oldest English-language theater.
www.mtc.mb.ca ✉ 174 Market Avenue ☎ 204/942-6537, 877/446-4500 (toll free in Manitoba) ◷ Oct–May

The North

Dawson City, Yukon
Palace Grand Theatre
Large, colorful opera house dating from 1899. Hosts the Gaslight Follies, recalling the Klondike Gold Rush.
✉ King Street ☎ 867/993-7200 ◷ Mid-May to Sep

Whitehorse, Yukon
Frantic Follies
A turn-of-the-20th-century vaudeville revue.
www.franticfollies.com
✉ Westmark Whitehorse Hotel, 201 Wood Street ☎ 867/668-2042 ◷ Late May to mid-Sep

Yukon Arts Centre
One of the few cultural venues in the vast and empty North. Regularly hosts world-class performers, international dance and theater companies, as well as classical recitals and concerts.
www.yukonartscentre.org
✉ 300 College Drive
☎ 867/667-8575 (and press 2) ◷ Year-round

Passion Play
It may seem surprising to find a thriving annual passion play in the depths of Alberta, but visit in mid-July and that's just what you will find. On a permanent site, close to Drumheller, the Badlands location bears an amazing resemblance to ancient Judaea, with a range of permanent structures providing a backdrop to a poignant portrayal of the life of Christ. The audience is seated above the stage set, around a superb natural amphitheater.
www.canadianpassionplay.com ✉ Box 457, Drumheller, west of town on South Dinosaur Trail ☎ 403/823-2001 ◷ Two weekends (Fri–Sun), mid-Jul

Nightlife

West Coast Comedy
Fans of improvisational comedy need look no further than the Vancouver Theatre Sports League, a highly entertaining company of comedians who base their shows on various spontaneous themes, including competitive improv.
www.vtsl.com ✉ New Revue Theatre, 1601 Johnston Street, Granville Island ☎ 604/738-7013; ◎ Wed–Sat

British Columbia & the Rockies

Jasper, Alberta
Atha-B Club
The liveliest dancing in town, plus live music most nights.
www.athabascahotel.com
✉ Athabasca Hotel, 510 Patricia Street ☎ 780/852-3386
◎ Daily 4pm–2am

Pete's on Patricia
One of the liveliest spots in Jasper. Live music and DJs.
✉ 614 Patricia Street ☎ 780/852-6262 ◎ Daily noon–2am

Vancouver, British Columbia
The Cellar
An intimate jazz club hosting some of the best local and touring jazz performers.
www.cellarjazz.com ✉ 3611 West Broadway ☎ 604/738-1959

Odyssey
Gay club also attracting a straight crowd for the latest dance music and dazzling drag shows.
www.theodysseynightclub.com
✉ 1251 Howe Street
☎ 604/689-5256 ◎ Daily 9pm–2am (also 2–4am Fri & Sat)

Plaza
Upscale, state-of-the-art dance club. Dress code applies Friday and Saturday.
www.plazaclub.net ✉ 881 Granville Street ☎ 604/646-0064
◎ Wed–Thu from 9pm, Fri–Sat from 8

Richards on Richards
A favorite nightclub and concert venue. International bands frequently appear.
www.richardsonrichards.com
✉ 1036 Richards Street
☎ 604/688-1099 ◎ Daily

The Pacific Coast

Victoria, British Columbia
Spinnakers
One of Canada's best brew-pubs.
✉ 308 Catherine Street
☎ 250/386-2739

The Prairies

Calgary, Alberta
Back Alley Nightclub
Great dance venue. Good old rock 'n' roll and local bands.
✉ 4630 MacLeod Trail SW
☎ 403/287-2500 ◎ Wed–Sat 7pm–2am

King Edward Hotel
The best place in town for rhythm and blues.
✉ 438 9th Avenue SE
☎ 403/262-1680 ◎ Mon–Sat 11am–2am

Edmonton, Alberta
Yardbird Suite
Great jazz from big-name performers.
www.yardbirdsuite.com ✉ 11 Tommy Banks Way ☎ 780/432-0428 ◎ Fri–Sat 8pm–1am, mid-Sep to Jun. Jam session Tue

Saskatoon, Saskatchewan
Crawdaddy's Louisiana Bar
New Orleans-style jazz, blues, Cajun and zydeco.
www.goforthegumbo.com
✉ 244 1st Avenue North ☎ 306/978-2729 ◎ Music Thu–Sat

The North

Dawson City, Yukon
Diamond Tooth Gertie's Gambling Hall
A Gold Rush-style saloon; Canada's oldest casino.
✉ Queen Street ☎ 867/993-5575 ◎ Daily 7pm–2am summer

Sports

British Columbia & the Rockies

Jasper, Alberta
Jasper Raft Tours
Rafting trips down the Athabasca River.
www.JasperRaftTours.com
✉ Box 398, Jasper, Alberta
☎ 780/852-2665, 1-888-55FLOAT
🕐 Mid-May to Sep

Vancouver, British Columbia
BC Lions
Canadian football under the world's biggest air-supported dome. Eight home games.
www.bclions.com ✉ BC Place Stadium, 777 Pacific Boulevard
☎ 604/661-3626 🕐 Late Jun–early Nov

Vancouver Canucks
Hockey at General Motors Place. Tickets sell out fast.
www.canucks.com ✉ General Motors Place, 800 Griffiths Way
☎ 604/899-7400; tickets: 604/899-7676 🕐 Sep–Mar

Whistler, British Columbia
Adult Ski School
Skiing courses for all ages and levels of expertise.
www.mywhistler.com
✉ Activity and Information Centre, Box 621 ☎ 604/938-2769, 877/991-9988 (toll free)
🕐 Daily, throughout winter

The Pacific Coast

Nanaimo, British Columbia
Ocean Explorers Diving
Explore artificial reefs and wrecks in clear waters; tuition and supplies.
✉ 1690 Stewart Avenue, Nanaimo ☎ 250/753-2055, 800/233-4145 (toll free in North America) 🕐 Year-round

The Prairies

Calgary, Alberta
Calgary Flames
One of the top teams in the National Hockey League.
www.calgaryflames.com
✉ Pengrowth Saddledome, 555 Saddledome Rise SE
☎ 403/777-2177 🕐 Oct–Apr

Calgary Stampeders
Canadian football at the McMahon Stadium.
www.stampeders.com
✉ McMahon Stadium, 1817 Crowchild Trail NW ☎ 403/289-0258 🕐 Late Jun–early Nov

Winnipeg, Manitoba
Assiniboia Downs
Thoroughbred racing, including Manitoba Derby.
www.assiniboiadowns.com
✉ 3975 Portage Avenue West
☎ 204/885-3330 🕐 May–Sep

The North

Dawson City, Yukon
Kodiak Wilderness Tours
Snowmobile, ATV, riverboat or canoe trips.
www.kodiaktours.ca ✉ Box 248, Dawson City ☎ 867/993-6333 🕐 Year-round

Top of the World Golf Course
Canada's most northerly course; superb scenery.
www.topoftheworldgolf.com
✉ Box 189, Dawson City
☎ 867/993-5888

Whitehorse, Yukon
Yukon Escapes
Standard and build-your-own trips, including ice fishing.
www.yukonescapes.com
✉ 4158 4th Avenue ☎ 867/668-6005 🕐 Year-round for various tours; some depend on season and weather conditions

Kitikmeot Northern Games
Traditional sports such as Alaskan hipkick and the one-arm reach take place during this three-day event in August, which also includes a northern feast. Locations change each year, and further information is available from Nunavut Tourism.
www.nunavuttourism.com
🚩 Nunavut Tourism
✉ Kitikmeot Region
☎ 867/979-6551, 866/686-2888

What's On When

Canada's Festival City
Competing with megacities Toronto, Montréal and Vancouver, the Alberta provincial capital emerged with the title "Canada's Festival City" because of its huge range of top-quality events. Every year Edmonton stages more than 30 events, many of international standing, including one of the best folk music festivals in the world, the biggest "alternative arts" festival in North America – the Edmonton International Fringe Festival – and the Klondike Days Festival, which attracts around 750,000 visitors.

January/February
Chinese New Year
Vancouver, British Columbia
A huge Chinese community celebrates in style here.
www.vancouverchinesegarden.com

February
Yukon Quest International Sled Dog Race
Whitehorse, Yukon
A 1,646-km (1,023-mile) race between Whitehorse and Fairbanks (Alaska).
www.yukonquest.com

March
Vancouver International Dance Festival
Vancouver, British Columbia
Nearly three weeks of shows featuring local, national and international dancers.
http://vidf.ca
Royal Manitoba Winter Fair
Brandon, Manitoba
Six-day agricultural show.
www.brandonfairs.com

April
Brant Wildlife Festival
Qualicum Beach, British Columbia
See more than 20,000 brant geese en route from Mexico to Alaska, with birdwatching, wildlife art and lectures.
www.brantfestival.bc.ca
World Ski and Snowboard Festival
Whistler, British Columbia
Ten days of action-packed events featuring Olympic and extreme sports legends.
www.wssf.com

May
Vancouver International Marathon
Vancouver, British Columbia
Not only the marathon but also many ancillary events.
www.adidasvanmarathon.ca

Vancouver International Children's Festival
Vancouver, British Columbia
Fun activities especially for children.
www.vancouverchildrensfestival.com

June/July
International Jazz Festival
Vancouver, British Columbia
Ten days of jazz, featuring world-class performers.
www.jazzvancouver.com

July
Calgary Stampede
Calgary, Alberta
► 72
www.calgary-stampede.com
Taste of Manitoba Food Festival
Winnipeg, Manitoba
Fine food and entertainment.
www.dinemanitoba.com

August
Folkorama
Winnipeg, Manitoba
Multicultural festival.
www.folklorama.ca

September
Vancouver Fringe Festival
Vancouver, British Columbia
Great theater – hilarious, mysterious, unusual shows.
www.vancouverfringe.com

November/December
North American Native Arts and Crafts Festival
Vancouver, British Columbia
Traditional performances, food and arts and crafts.

November
Canadian Finals Rodeo and Farmfair International
Edmonton, Alberta
Canada's toughest rodeo stars battle for the title; also huge agricultural show.
www.canadianfinalsrodeo.ca

Practical Matters

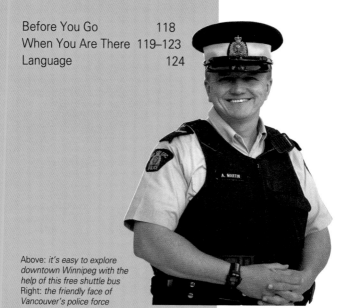

Above: *it's easy to explore downtown Winnipeg with the help of this free shuttle bus*
Right: *the friendly face of Vancouver's police force*

TIME DIFFERENCES

GMT
12 noon

Vancouver
← 5am

New York
← 7am

Germany
→ 1pm

Spain
→ 1pm

Sydney
→ 10pm

BEFORE YOU GO

WHAT YOU NEED

		UK	USA	Europe
● Required	Some countries require a passport to remain valid for a minimum period (usually at least six months) beyond the date of entry – contact their consulate or embassy or your travel agency for details.			
Passport		●	○	●
Visa (regulations can change – check before booking your journey)		▲	▲	▲
Return Ticket		○	○	○
Health Inoculation		●	▲	●
Travel Insurance		○	○	○
Drivers' License		●	●	●
Car Insurance Certificate		●	●	●
Car Registration Documentation		●	●	●

● Required ○ Suggested ▲ Not required

WHEN TO GO

Vancouver

██████ High season

▭ Low season

6°C	7°C	11°C	14°C	17°C	21°C	23°C	22°C	19°C	14°C	9°C	6°C
JAN	FEB	MAR	APR	MAY	JUN	JUL	AUG	SEP	OCT	NOV	DEC
Wet	Wet	Wet	Wet	Sunshine & showers	Sun	Sun	Sun	Sunshine & showers	Sunshine & showers	Wet	Wet

☀ Sun   ☁ Cloud   🌧 Wet   🌦 Sunshine & showers

TOURIST OFFICES

In the UK
Canadian Tourism Commission
✉ Visit Canada, PO Box 170, Ashford, Kent TN24 0ZX
☎ (0906) 871 5000

In the USA
Canadian Tourism Commission
✉ 550 South Hope Street, 9th Floor Los Angeles, CA 90071-2627 USA
☎ 323/937-7021
Fax: 323/937-5657

Canadian Tourism Commission
✉ 2625 Piedmont Road, Suite 56–333 Atlanta, GA 30324 USA
☎ 404/315-0028
Fax: 404/315-4801

In Australia
Canadian Tourism Commission
✉ Suite 105, Jones Bay Wharf, 19–21 Pirrama Road, Pyrmont, NSW 2009
☎ (02) 9571-1655
Fax: (02) 9571-1766

EMERGENCY TELEPHONE NUMBERS
For police, fire department and ambulance services:
In Manitoba, Saskatchewan, Alberta and mainland British Columbia : ☎ 911
In Vancouver Island, Yukon, Northwest Territories and Nunavut :
☎ 0 for operator and say that it is an emergency.

WHEN YOU ARE THERE

ARRIVING

The major airports of Western Canada are Vancouver, Calgary, Edmonton and Winnipeg. Most visitors will arrive at one of them. There are also smaller airports in Regina, Saskatoon, Yellowknife, Whitehorse and Iqaluit. The national airline is Air Canada (☎ 888/247-2262; www.aircanada.ca).

Vancouver International Airport
15km (9.3 miles) south of downtown, Car or cab – 30 min (depending on traffic), Airporter bus – 45 min
Calgary International Airport
16km (10 miles) north of downtown, Car or cab – 30 min, Airporter bus – 45 min
Edmonton International Airport
30km (18.5 miles) south of downtown, Car or cab – 35–40 min, Airporter bus – 45 min
Winnipeg International Airport
6.5km (4 miles) west of downtown, Car or cab – 20 min (longer in heavy traffic), Regular city bus – 30 min

MONEY

Canada's currency is the Canadian dollar (100 cents = $1). Bills come in $5, $10, $20, $50 and $100, but the $100 is often difficult to use – people are suspicious of it due to forgeries. Coins come as pennies (1 cent), nickels (5 cents), dimes (10 cents), quarters (25 cents), loonies ($1 – named for the bird on them) and twonies ($2). The $1 coin is gold colored, the $2 coin has a gold center and silver rim.
Exchange rates are notoriously variable so it is wise to check the current rate just before leaving on a trip. In May 2004, the rates were: Can$1 = US$0.76 ; UK£0.46; 1.10 Australian dollars; 0.65 euros.

TIME

There are four time zones in the region – Eastern (GMT+5), Central (+6), Mountain (+7) and Pacific (+8). For daylight saving time, clocks go forward one hour on first Sun in Apr and back last Sun Oct. Saskatchewan uses daylight saving time all year.

CUSTOMS

YES From any country, you may bring the following into Western Canada provided you are over 18:

200 cigarettes, 50 cigars or 400 grams of tobacco.
1 liter bottle of wine or spirits
24 regular sized cans or bottles of beer
Dogs, cats and other pets – but they must have been vaccinated against rabies within the preceding 12-month period and you must carry the vaccination certificate with you.

NO Plants, flowers or other vegetation, Illegal drugs, obscene material, firearms and ammunition – except in certain specific cases (hunting trips, etc) when you must carry supporting documentation (details of weapon and ammunition, details of hunting trip, etc).

More information on restrictions or regulations can be obtained from Revenue Canada, Customs and Excise, Ottawa K1A 0L5 (www.ccra-adrc.gc.ca).

EMBASSIES (located in Canadian Federal capital of Ottawa)

 USA
613-238-5335
www.usembassy
canada.gov

 UK
613-237-1530
www.britainin-
canada.org

 AUSTRALIA
613-236-0841
www.ahc-
ottawa.org

 FRANCE
613-789-1795
www.amba
france-ca.org

 GERMANY
613-232-1101
www.germanem-
bassyottawa.org

WHEN YOU ARE THERE

TOURIST OFFICES

- **Travel Alberta**
  ✉ PO Box 2500,
  Edmonton, AB T5J 2Z4
  ☎ 800/252-3782;
  www.discoveralberta.com

- **Tourism British Columbia**
  ✉ Parliament Buildings,
  Victoria, BC V8V 1XA
  ☎ 800/663-6000;
  www.hellobc.com

- **Travel Manitoba**
  ✉ 7th Floor, 155 Carlton
  Street, Winnipeg,
  MN R3C 3H8
  ☎ 800/665-0040;
  www.travelmanitoba.com

- **Northwest Territories
  Tourism**
  ✉ PO Box 610,
  Yellowknife, NWT X1A 2N5
  ☎ 800/661-0788;
  www.explorenwt.com

- **Nunavut Tourism**
  ✉ PO Box 1450, Iqaluit,
  NU X0A 0H0
  ☎ 866/686-2888;
  www.nunavuttourism.com

- **Tourism Saskatchewan**
  ✉ 1922 Park Street,
  Regina, SK S4P 3V7
  ☎ 800/667-7191;
  www.sasktourism.com

- **Tourism Yukon**
  ✉ PO Box 2703,
  Whitehorse, YK Y1A 2C6
  ☎ 800/661-0494;
  www.touryukon.com

PUBLIC HOLIDAYS

National Holidays:

1 Jan	New Year's Day
Mar/Apr	Good Friday
May	(Mon closest to 24) Victoria Day
July 1	Canada Day
Sep	(1st Mon) Labour Day
Oct	(2nd Mon) Thanksgiving (note: not same date as US Thanksgiving)
Dec 25	Christmas Day

Provincial/Territorial Holidays:

April 1	Nunavut Day (Nunavut)
Aug	(1st Mon) Heritage Day (AB); British Columbia Day (BC); Civic Holiday (MB, SK, NWT, Nunavut)
Aug	(3rd Mon) Discovery Day (YK)

Other holidays celebrated:

Mar/Apr	Easter Monday
Nov 11	Remembrance Day
Dec 26	Boxing Day

OPENING HOURS

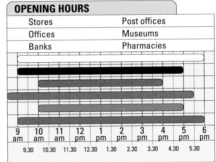

Stores	Post offices
Offices	Museums
Banks	Pharmacies

9 am (9.30) · 10 am (10.30) · 11 am (11.30) · 12 pm (12.30) · 1 pm (1.30) · 2 pm (2.30) · 3 pm (3.30) · 4 pm (4.30) · 5 pm (5.30) · 6 pm

Stores 9am–6pm Mon–Fri (until 9pm Thu and Fri) 9am–5pm
Sat, noon–5pm Sun. Some stores do not open on Sun.
Supermarkets and malls open longer. **Offices** 9am–5pm
(4pm government offices). Many have flexible hours
especially in the large cities. **Banks** 10am–4pm Mon–Fri .
Some branches open earlier and some stay open to 5 or
6pm on Thu or Fri. **Post Offices** 8.30am–5.30pm Mon–Fri.
Some convenience stores sell stamps and may be open
later than 5.30pm and on Sat morning. **Museums** 10 or
11am–5pm. Most are closed Mon. Major museums stay
open until 9pm one evening a week. **Pharmacies** Mon–Fri
9am–6pm, Sat 9am–5pm, Sun noon–5pm. Major cities have
pharmacies open 24-hours a day. **Attractions** Opening
hours of tourist sites vary seasonally. Outside major cities,
many are closed between mid-Oct and mid-May.

DRIVE ON THE RIGHT

RESTROOMS FREE

★★ ★★

PUBLIC TRANSPORT

 Internal Flights Air Canada (and subsidiaries Jazz and Tango) is the major carrier, servicing every province and territory, with a monopoly on many routes (☎ 888/247-2262; www.aircanada.ca). WestJet provides budget air service in Western Canada (☎ 403/250-5839; toll free 888/937-8538 or 800/538-5696 www.westjet.com).

 Trains Much of the rail passenger service is provided by VIA Rail (☎ 888/VIA-RAIL; www.viarail.ca). Trains are clean, fast and efficient, and are a pleasant and scenic way to see the country. In addition, scenic tours are provided on the Rocky Mountaineer and Skeena trains (☎ 604/606-7245 or 877/460-3200; www.rkymtnrail.com)

Long Distance Buses Relatively inexpensive buses give access to most of the region. The major company is Greyhound Canada (☎ 800/661-8747; www.greyhound.ca), with cross-border links to US cities. A Canada Discovery Pass is available for differing lengths of time, and savings on tickets purchased in advance are considerable.

Ferries BC Ferries are the main operators on the Pacific coast (☎ 888/223-3779; www.bcferries.bc.ca), including the Inside Passage service (➤ 58). Three services link the US west coast and BC: Black Ball Transport (☎ 250/386-2202); Clipper Navigation (☎ 800/888-2535 or 250/382-8100); and San Juan Cruises (☎ 360/738-8099).

Urban Transport In general, all cities in Western Canada have good public trans-portation systems that make travel relatively easy for visitors. The Vancouver Translink system (☎ 604/953-3333; www.translink.bc.ca) includes buses, trolleys, the SeaBus catamaran ferries and the above-ground Skytrain rail service.

CAR RENTAL

 All major car rental firms are represented here. To rent, you must be over 21, with ID and a valid driver's license, held for at least a year. You will need a credit card, and to return the vehicle to another site, a sizeable drop-off fee will apply.

TAXIS

 Taxis are the most costly way to travel. Fares mount quickly especially in rush-hour traffic in the cities. Cabs can be found in stands beside major hotels, at airports, train and bus stations. They can also be hailed on the street or called by telephone.

DRIVING

 Speed limits on expressways: 100kph (60mph)

 Speed limits on other major roads: 70–90kph (40–55mph)

 Speed limits in urban areas and on rural routes: 50kph (30mph) or less

 Must be worn by all persons in a vehicle (drivers and passengers) in both the front and back seats.

 Random breath-testing. Never drive under the influence of alcohol.

 Unleaded gas is sold by the liter (leaded gas has been phased out). Gas stations are plentiful on major routes and approaches to cities and stay open until 9 or 10pm (some stay open all night). Away from urban areas, and especially in the North, they may be far apart

 If you plan on driving in remote areas, it is wise to join the Canadian Automobile Assoc-iation (☎ 800/222-4357; www.caa.ca), who can help in case of breakdown. Card-carrying members of the AAA are entitled to full service with the CAA. Most rental companies provide a rescue service. In case of an emergency, call 911 or 0, depending on your location (➤ 119) .

121

Ruler markings

CENTIMETERS
0 1 2 3 4 5 6 7 8

INCHES
0 1 2 3

PERSONAL SAFETY

Although Western Canada is remarkably crime-free, a few simple precautions will help prevent unfortunate incidents.

- don't leave bags or other valuables visible in your car, stow them in the trunk
- don't wear expensive jewelry and carry large sums of money
- in major cities, where there may be pickpockets, carry credit cards and passports in a pouch or belt
- walk only along well-lit streets at night

The Royal Canadian Mounted Police (RCMP) is the federal police force (www.rcmp-grc.gc.ca) and they ensure regular police work in all four Western provinces and in the three territories. On duty, officers look just like any other police force and drive cars (red jackets, Stetsons and horses are only used on ceremonial occasions). All of the major cities have their own police forces in addition to the RCMP.

Police assistance: ☎ 911 except Vancouver Island, Yukon, Northwest Territories and Nunavut : ☎ 0 for the operator instead and say that it is an emergency.

ELECTRICITY

Voltage in Canada is 110v (same as US). Sockets require plugs with two (maybe three)

flat prongs. Visitors from outside North America need an adaptor, on sale at most airports and travel stores in Canada (but better purchased in advance). Razors, hairdriers and laptops are usually dual-voltage, but correct plugs are required.

TELEPHONES

Outdoor public telephones are located in glass and metal booths. To make a call, lift the handset, insert the correct coin (25¢ or $1 coins), a telephone credit card or a prepaid calling card (available in post offices, convenience stores, newsagents, etc), and then dial.

International Dialing Codes	
From Western Canada to:	
USA:	1
UK:	011 44
Australia:	011 61
France:	011 33
Germany:	011 49
Italy:	011 39
Netherlands:	011 31
Spain:	011 34

POST

Mail boxes are generally red with the words Canada Post/ Postes Canada written on them. For hours of post offices ➤ 120. Cost of stamps (as of May 2004):
• minimum of 49¢ to mail a regular letter within Canada
• minimum of 80¢ to send it across the border to the US
• minimum of $1.40 to send it overseas.

TIPS/GRATUITIES

Yes ✓ No ✗		
Restaurants (where service not included)	✓	10–15%
Cafés (where service not included)	✓	10%
Hotel service staff	✓	10%
Hairdressers	✓	10%
Taxis	✓	10%
Tour guides	✓	$1
Cinema attendants	✗	
Cloakroom attendants	✓	$1
Washrooms/restrooms	✗	

PHOTOGRAPHY

The best light for photography is generally early morning or evening. Be careful with lighting when taking photos in the snow of winter. The reflections of the sun on the snow can be incredibly bright.

Where to buy film: many convenience stores and pharmacies will sell regular film in addition to specialized camera stores.

Restrictions: certain museums will not allow photography at all and practically all forbid the use of flash.

HEALTH

Canada's excellent health system is free for Canadians, but foreigners must pay, and even simple procedures can be expensive. It is advisable to arrange full health coverage, including a "repatriation" clause in case no suitable treatment is available. Your own insurance company is the best source for advice. Keep all bills and receipts to make a claim.

Dental care is also excellent but costly, so include this in your insurance. Most hotels can recommend a dentist, which can save time, or try the tourist office or Yellow Pages. Again, keep all documentation for your claim.

The Prairies have hot summers, with temperatures up into the 30s°C (mid-80s°F). Use sunscreen and wear sunglasses. These are needed in the North too, where it's surprisingly bright (with 24-hour sunshine in summer); in winter the reflection off the snow can cause serious sunburn.

Carry a full supply of any prescription drug that you have to take. Over-the-counter drugs are readily available in pharmacies, but no Canadian pharmacy will accept an out-of-province prescription. Should you run out of or lose your supply, you will have to visit a Canadian doctor and get a new prescription that's recognized locally. There will be costs involved for this.

It is safe to drink tap water in any part of Canada. Bottled water is also widely available. When camping, though, boil your drinking water for 10 minutes as protection against "Beaver fever" (unpleasant, but it only lasts a few days), caused by a parasite found in lakes and streams.

CONCESSIONS

Students Full-time students (and the term can include grade-school age) can get certain reductions at museums and other tourist attractions. Carry your student card or be prepared to prove your age.

Seniors Most museums and tourist attractions offer reduced rates for seniors. Some consider a person a senior at 55, others at 60 and yet others at 65. So if this affects you, it is best to ask. Here again, you will have to be prepared to prove your age. Public transportation systems offer reductions for seniors too, but in some cities this only applies to local residents. Once again, you will have to ask.

CLOTHING SIZES

UK	Rest of Europe	Canada/USA	
36	46	36	
38	48	38	
40	50	40	
42	52	42	Suits
44	54	44	
46	56	46	
7	41	8	
7.5	42	8.5	
8.5	43	9.5	
9.5	44	10.5	Shoes
10.5	45	11.5	
11	46	12	
14.5	37	14.5	
15	38	15	
15.5	39/40	15.5	
16	41	16	Shirts
16.5	42	16.5	
17	43	17	
8	34	6	
10	36	8	
12	38	10	
14	40	12	Dresses
16	42	14	
18	44	16	
4.5	38	6	
5	38	6.5	
5.5	39	7	
6	39	7.5	Shoes
6.5	40	8	
7	41	8.5	

WHEN DEPARTING

- Call your airline two days before departure to reconfirm your flight and check that details are unchanged.
- For international flights, arrive at the airport two hours before take-off (or ask your airline for guidance).
- Remember that lines to pass through security can be long at major airports and that people have missed flights by arriving with too little time for this procedure.

LANGUAGE

Canada is officially a bilingual English/French country. This means that all services of the Federal Government are offered in both languages. You will notice this particularly at Canadian Customs, in post offices and in the National Parks. There are French-speaking communities in all four Western provinces, but they are quite small compared with the large number of French speakers in Eastern Canada. You will not need to learn any French while traveling in Western Canada.

Inuktitut is the language of the Inuit peoples of the Northwest Territories and Nunavut. Although it has been spoken for thousands of years, Inuktitut has only been written relatively recently. In the NWT (western and central Arctic), Roman orthography is used. In Nunavut (eastern Arctic), Inuktitut is written using symbols called syllabics to represent different sounds. The word Nunavut (pronounced noo-na-voot) means "Our Land."

Here are a few useful Inuktitut expressions using Roman orthography:

ENGLISH	INUKTITUT	PRONUNCIATION
How are you?	Qanuipit?	(Ka-nwee-peet?)
I'm fine	Qanuingittunga	(Ka-nweeng-ni-toon-ga)
What's your name?	Kinauvit?	(Kee-nau-veet?)
Thank you	Qujannamiik	(Coo-yan-na-mee-ick)
You're welcome	Ilaali	(Ee-lah-lih)
Yes	Ii	(Ee)
No	Aakka or aagaa	(Ah-ka or Ah-ga)
Maybe	Atsuuli or aamai	(At-soo-lee or Ah-my)
(I don't really know)		
How much is it?	Qatsituqqa?	(Cat-see-to-kaw?)
How many?	Qatsiit?	(Cat-seet?)
Expensive	Akitujuq	(Ah-kee-too-yuk)
Did you make this?	Una sanajait?	(Oo-na san-ai-yate?)
What is it?	Una suna?	(Oo-na soo-na?)
I'm cold	Qiuliqtunga	(K-o-lick-toon-ga)
It's cold (weather)	Ikkiirnaqtuq	(Ick-eang-nak-took)
Will the weather be good today?	Silasianguniapa?	(See-la-see-aang-un-ee-aa-pa?)
I'm hungry	Kaaktunga	(Kak-toon-ga)
Help!	Ikajunga!	(Ick-a-yung-ga!)
I'm sick	Aaniajunga	(Ah-nee-a-yung-ga)
Where am I?	Namiippunga?	(Nah-me-poon-ga?)
Where's the hotel?	Nau taima sinitavik?	(Naowk tie-ma see-nee-ta-vik?)
Where's the store?	Nau taima niuvivik?	(Naowk tie-ma new-vee-vik?)
Where's the church?	Nau taima tuksiavik?	(Naowk tie-ma took-see-aa-vik?)
I'd like to telephone	Uqaalagumajunga	(Oo-ka-la-goo-ma-jung-ga)
I'd like to go fishing	Iqalliarumajunga	(Ee-ka-lee-aa-roo-ma-jung-ga)
I'd like to go by dogteam	Qimuksikkuurumavunga	(Kim-mook-sick-koo-roo-mah-voon-ga)
I'd like to take your photo	Ajjiliurumajagit	(A-jee-lee-oo-roo-maa-ya-geet)
I'd like to use the washroom	Quisuktunga	(Kwee-soot-toon-ga)
Goodbye (to one person)	Tavvauvutit	(Tah-vow-voo-teet)
Goodbye (to a group)	Tavvauvusi	(Tah-vow-voo-see)

INDEX

Acknowledgements
The Automobile Association would like to thank the following libraries, agencies and photographers for their assistance in the preparation of this title.

ALAMY 6c, 9c, 58c; ANDREW DORAN/www.coastphoto.com 18b; CALGARY STAMPEDE 9b, 72b; DEPARTMENT OF TOURISM AND CULTURE, YUKON 90b; GETTY IMAGES 7c; MENNONITE VILLAGE 65c; PHOTODISC 12b; REX FEATURES 14c, 14b; TOURISM VANCOUVER 30/31; YUKON BERINGIA CENTRE 86c

The remaining photographs are held in the Association's own library (AA WORLD TRAVEL LIBRARY) with contributions from the following:
PETE BENNETT 1, 21c, 21b, 24c, 27b, 30c, 36b, 43b, 45ct, 47c, 51b, 54c, 55b, 59, 60, 61, 62t, 62b, 63t, 63b, 64tl, 64tc, 65t, 66, 67t, 67c, 69t, 69c,70t, 71t, 72t, 73t, 73c, 74t, 74c, 75t, 75c, 76t, 76b, 77t, 77b, 78t, 78c, 79t, 79c, 89b, 117b; CHRIS COE 2, 10b, 13t, 13ct, 13c, 14t, 15, 16b, 17t, 18t, 19c, 20t, 21t, 22t, 22/23, 23t, 24t, 25t, 26t, 27t, 31c, 35, 39, 40, 46b, 56, 57c, 70b, 71ct, 80, 81t, 81c, 82, 83, 84t, 84b, 85, 86t, 87t, 87b, 88t, 88c, 89t, 90t; MICHAEL DENT 23c, 38c, 49, 50, 51t, 52t, 52b, 53, 54t, 55t, 55ct, 57t, 58t, 71cb, 71b, 91-116; CLIVE SAWYER 5, 6t, 6b, 7t, 7b, 8t, 8c, 9t, 10t, 11t, 12t, 17c, 19b, 20b, 22c, 23b, 25b, 26c, 28, 29, 30t, 31t, 33, 36t, 37, 38t, 41, 42t, 42b, 43t, 44t, 44c, 45t, 47t, 68, 117t, 122t, 112b; PETER TIMMERMANS 8b, 26b, 32, 34, 48, 70c

AAA Questionnaire

Dear Traveler

Your comments, opinions and recommendations are very important to us. So please help us to improve our travel guides by taking a few minutes to complete this simple questionnaire.

Send to: Essential Guides,
MailStop 66, 1000 AAA Drive, Heathrow, FL 32746–5063

Your recommendations...

We always encourage readers' recommendations for restaurants, nightlife or shopping – if your recommendation is added to the next edition of the guide, we will send you a FREE AAA Essential Guide of your choice. Please state below the establishment name, location and your reasons for recommending it.

_____

_____

_____

_____

_____

Please send me AAA Essential _____

About this guide...

Which title did you buy?

_____ **AAA Essential**

Where did you buy it?_____

When? m m / y y

Why did you choose a AAA Essential Guide?_____

_____

_____

Did this guide meet with you expectations?

Exceeded ☐   Met all ☐   Met most ☐   Fell below ☐

Please give your reasons _____

_____

_____

_____

continued on next page...

Were there any aspects of this guide that you particularly liked? ______

______

______

______

______

______

Is there anything we could have done better? ______

______

______

______

______

______

About you...

Name (Mr/Mrs/Ms) ______

Address ______

______

______ Zip ______

Daytime tel nos. ______

Which age group are you in?

Under 25 ☐ 25–34 ☐ 35–44 ☐ 45–54 ☐ 55–64 ☐ 65+ ☐

How many trips do you make a year?

Less than one ☐ One ☐ Two ☐ Three or more ☐

Are you a AAA member? Yes ☐ No ☐

Name of AAA club ______

About your trip

When did you book? m m / y y When did you travel? m m / y y

How long did you stay? ______

Was it for business or leisure? ______

Did you buy any other travel guides for your trip? Yes ☐ No ☐

If yes, which ones? ______

______

Thank you for taking the time to complete this questionnaire.

All information is for AAA internal use only and will not be distributed outside the organization to any third parties.

The Atlas

	Toll Motorway (Turnpike)
	Motorway
	National road
	Other road
	International boundary
	Administrative region boundary
■	City
▪	Town
	National park
■	Place of interest
✈	Airport
³³⁶³▲	Height in metres
=	Mountain pass

0   300 km
0   200 miles

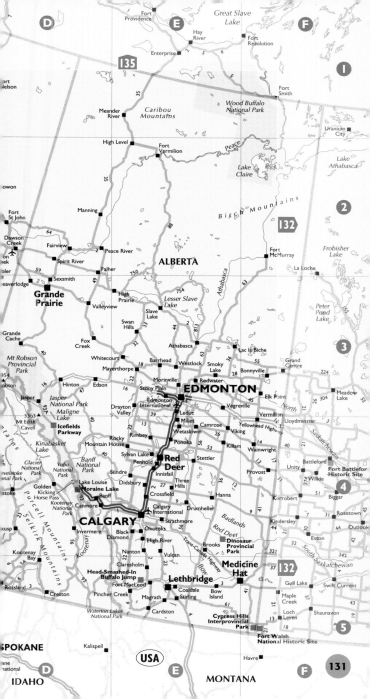

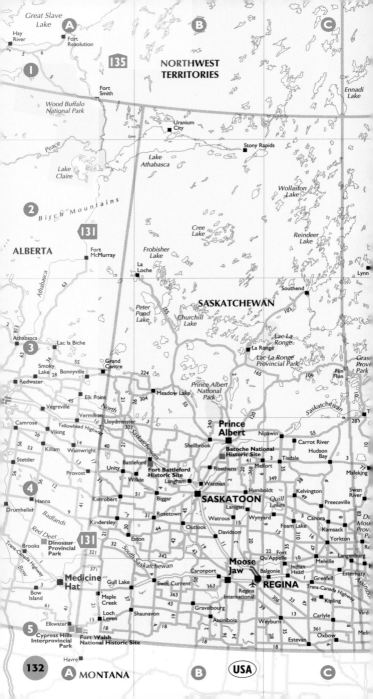

*Beaufort
Sea*

Sachs
Harbour ■

*Banks
Island*

toyaktuk

*Cape
Parry*

*Amundsen
Gulf*

Holman ■

*Victoria
Island*

kluk Nogait
ational Park

Paulatuk ■

2

ort
od Hope

Kugluktuk ■
(Coppermine)

Coronation Gulf

*Franklin
Mountains*

*Great Bear
Lake*

Port ■
Radium

NUNAVUT

*Contwoyto
Lake*

3

enzie

NORTHWEST TERRITORIES

Wrigley ■

a i n s

4

Rae-Edzo ■

Yellowknife ■
✈
Yellowknife ■

Fort ■
Simpson

Liard

Fort ■
Providence

*Great Slave
Lake*

Hay ■
River

Fort ■
Resolution

Enterprise ■

5

son

Meander ■
River

*Caribou
Mountains*

Fort
Smith

*Wood Buffalo
National Park*

Uranium City

Sight Locator Index

This index relates to the atlas section on pages 129–135. We have given map references to the main sights of interest in the book. Some sights in the index may not be plotted on the atlas. **Note: ibc – inside back cover.**

For the main index see pages 125–26